D1381331

MY SEC RET

MY SECRET

ALSO BY FRANK WARREN
POSTSECRET

A POSTSECRET BOOK

MY SECRET

COMPILED BY FRANK WARREN

Copyright © Frank Warren 2007

The right of Frank Warren to be identified as
the author of this work has been asserted by him in accordance with the
Copyright, Designs and Patents Act 1988.

First published in hardback in Great Britain in 2007 by
Orion Books
an imprint of the Orion Publishing Group Ltd
Orion House, 5 Upper St Martin's Lane,
London WC2H 9EA
An Hachette Livre UK Company

3 5 7 9 10 8 6 4 2

All rights reserved. Apart from any use permitted under UK copyright law, this publication may only be reproduced, stored or transmitted, in any form, or by any means, with prior permission in writing of the publishers or, in the case of reprographic production, in accordance with the terms of licences issued by the Copyright Licensing Agency.

A CIP catalogue record for this book is available
from the British Library.

ISBN: 978 0 7528 8987 0

Printed in Spain by Cayfosa-Quebecor

The Orion Publishing Group's policy is to use papers that are natural, renewable and recyclable and made from wood grown in sustainable forests. The logging and manufacturing processes are expected to conform to the environmental regulations of the country of origin.

Every effort has been made to fulfil requirements with regard to reproducing copyright material. The author and publisher will be glad to rectify any omissions at the earliest opportunity.

www.orionbooks.co.uk

This book is dedicated to my daughter, and every other young person making that journey from the home they were born into toward the home they will create for themselves.

–Frank

FOREWORD

Frank Warren and the PostSecret community changed my life as founder of 1-800-SUICIDE.

In 1998, I founded the Kristin Brooks Hope Center and 1-800-SUICIDE in memory of my wife, Kristin, whom I lost to suicide triggered by postpartum depression following the stillbirth of our infant son. In January 2005, as we approached our two millionth call, all federal funds ended—seriously threatening the future of 1-800-SUICIDE. At a time when I finally had reason to hope I was making a difference, the threat of losing the hotline felt like I was losing Kristin again.

Earlier this year, Frank posted a plea for support on the PostSecret website. The outpouring from PostSecret readers was immediate and overwhelming. In just over one week, more than $30,000 was raised from over nine hundred contributors. Without the help of Frank and the PostSecret community, the nation would have lost an eight-year-old resource that has been connecting callers from fifty states to help and hope.

It has been a privilege to work with PostSecret and be a part of this healing process.

—Reese Butler

INTRODUCTION

In the past two years, I have received more than fifty thousand secrets mailed to me on artfully decorated postcards. Most secrets are sent anonymously, but the secrets that arrive from young people usually stand out; their passions run deeper, their loneliness feels more desolate, their joy is expansive. Their postcards reveal a hidden landscape and sound as though they come from brave explorers finding their way through a wilderness.

When I travel to college campuses and speak about the PostSecret Project with students, I have been inspired by the stories they have told me, stories that begin with a secret and end with hope. A young man in Seattle described how he gave his mother a copy of PostSecret as a gift, and how the secrets inside allowed them to discuss experiences and concerns they had never talked about before.

In Maryland, at the end of a talk, a courageous young woman stood up and showed all of us the T-shirt she designed that exposed the eating disorder she had hidden. On the front it read, *20% of all anorexics will die,* and on the back it listed the symptoms of the disease. "When I made my shirt and wore it to school, I was nervous to find out how my friends would react," she said, "but when my classmates saw it, they supported me and even asked me to make shirts like mine for them to wear too."

A woman in New York was emboldened to leave her abusive fiancé and remake her life after she recognized a secret she was keeping from herself on a stranger's postcard.

A teacher in Chicago told me that she displayed a "Veil of Secrets" at her school—a patchwork of more than three hundred postcards she collected from students. "It got students talking and caused people to feel more connected." She went on to tell me that it exasperated certain administrators, who removed it and declared, *What state standards could possibly support such gratuitous and sophomoric impulses?* (I went to high school in Illinois. I wish I had been lucky enough to have been in her class.)

Sometimes when I am on the road and feeling lost or lonely, I write a postcard home. Sharing my thoughts and feelings on a card usually helps me feel a little better. But what makes me feel more connected is imagining my card finding its way home and being placed in my mailbox by my favorite mail carrier. She groups the PostSecret cards into a stack a few inches high and then carefully secures the pile by wrapping two rubber bands around it, like a gift wrapped in a ribbon.

And that is how I imagine my postcard, bound together with everyone else's.

—Frank Warren

See me

Post Secret
13345 Copper Ridge Rd.
German town, Maryland
Usa 20874-3454

Truth is....
2(x)ist
2(x)ist
I don't like sex.

FOR SOME REASON, I KNOW I WILL DIE YOUNG...
AND IT SCARES ME A LITTLE BIT.

I HATE THIS
TOWN BUT I'M
SO AFRAID TO
LEAVE

I wish guys
loved me like
they love my
FRIENDS

PostSecret
13345 Copper
Ridge Rd
Germantown, MD
USA 20874-3454

My Dreams are
Bigger
than this Small
Apartment

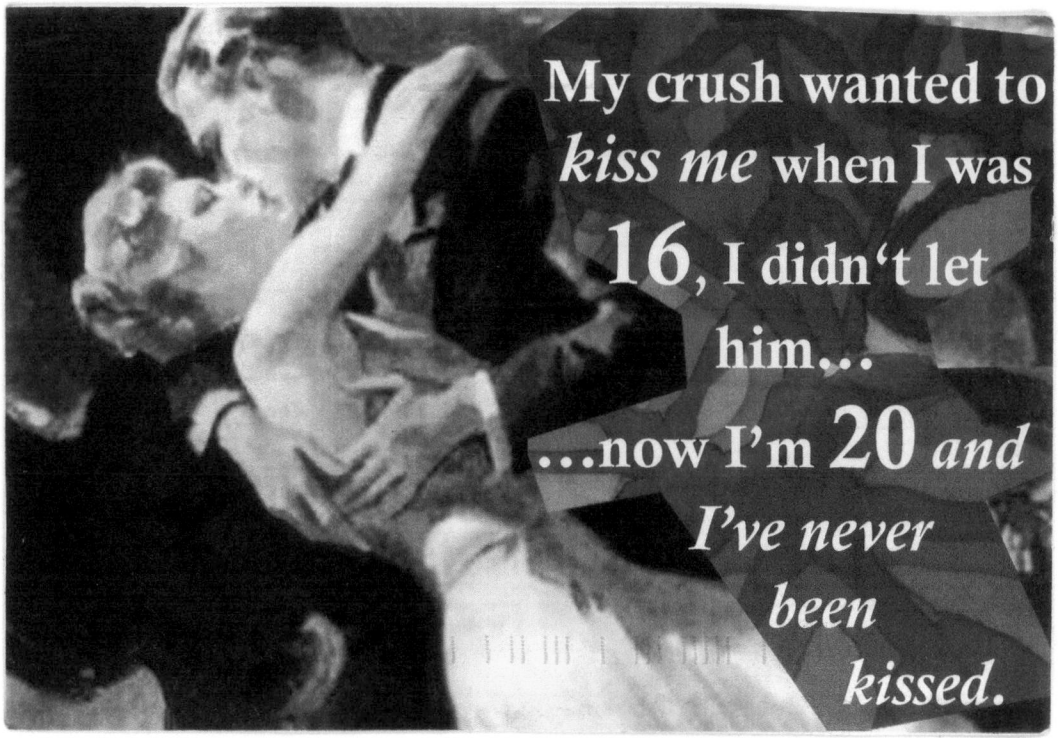
My crush wanted to
kiss me when I was
16, I didn't let
him...
...now I'm 20 *and*
I've never
been
kissed.

9,898
STUDENTS
AND I VE NEVER FELT MORE ALONE

I wish I had not tried to grow up so fast. I feel like I missed some important parts of young adulthood.

He left me anyway.

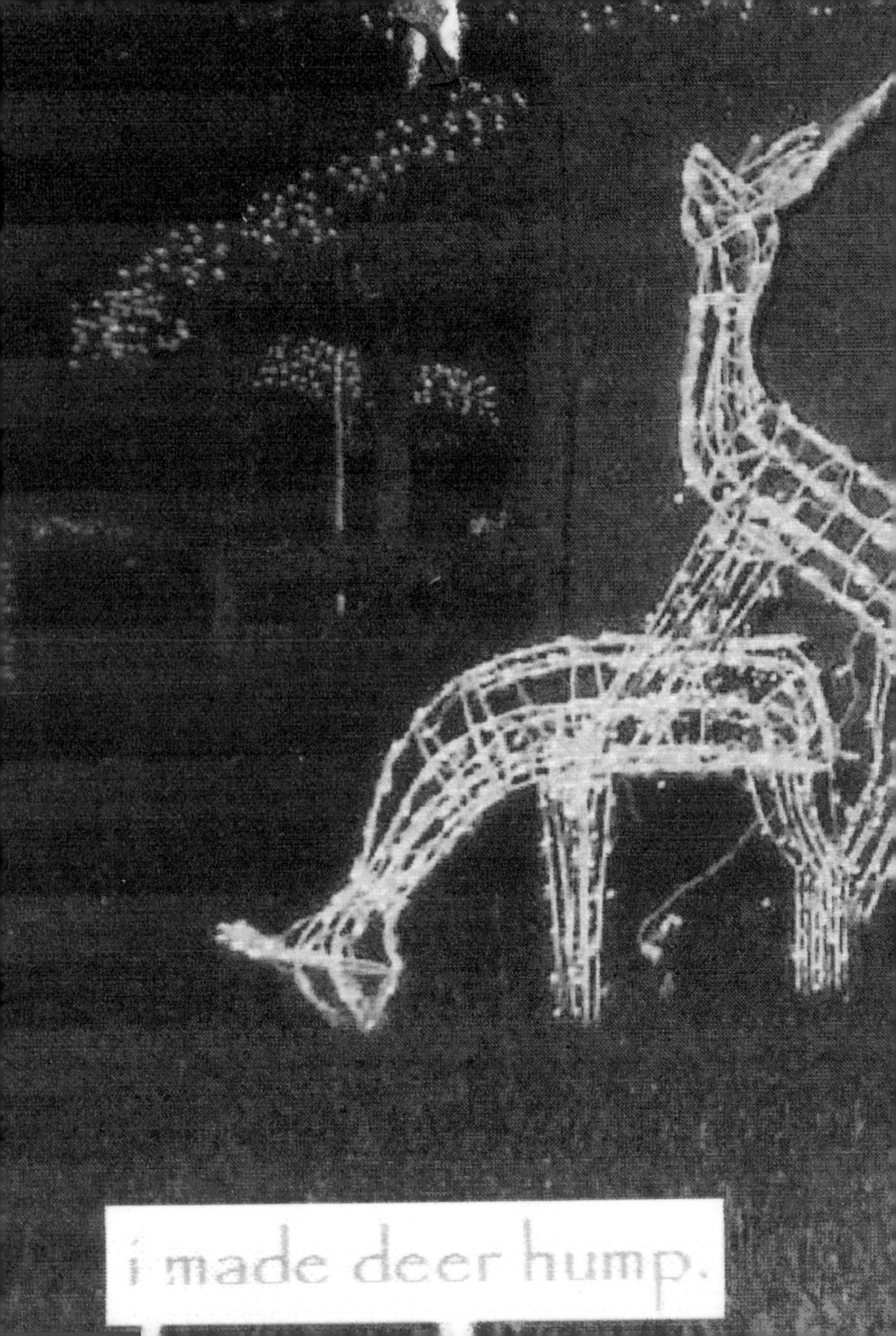
i made deer hump.

I'm forced to carry your secret because you were too weak to keep it to yourself.

I Believe in my Childhood
Dreams
Vuan

We haven't spoken
since that night.
It was an accident.
I SWEAR!

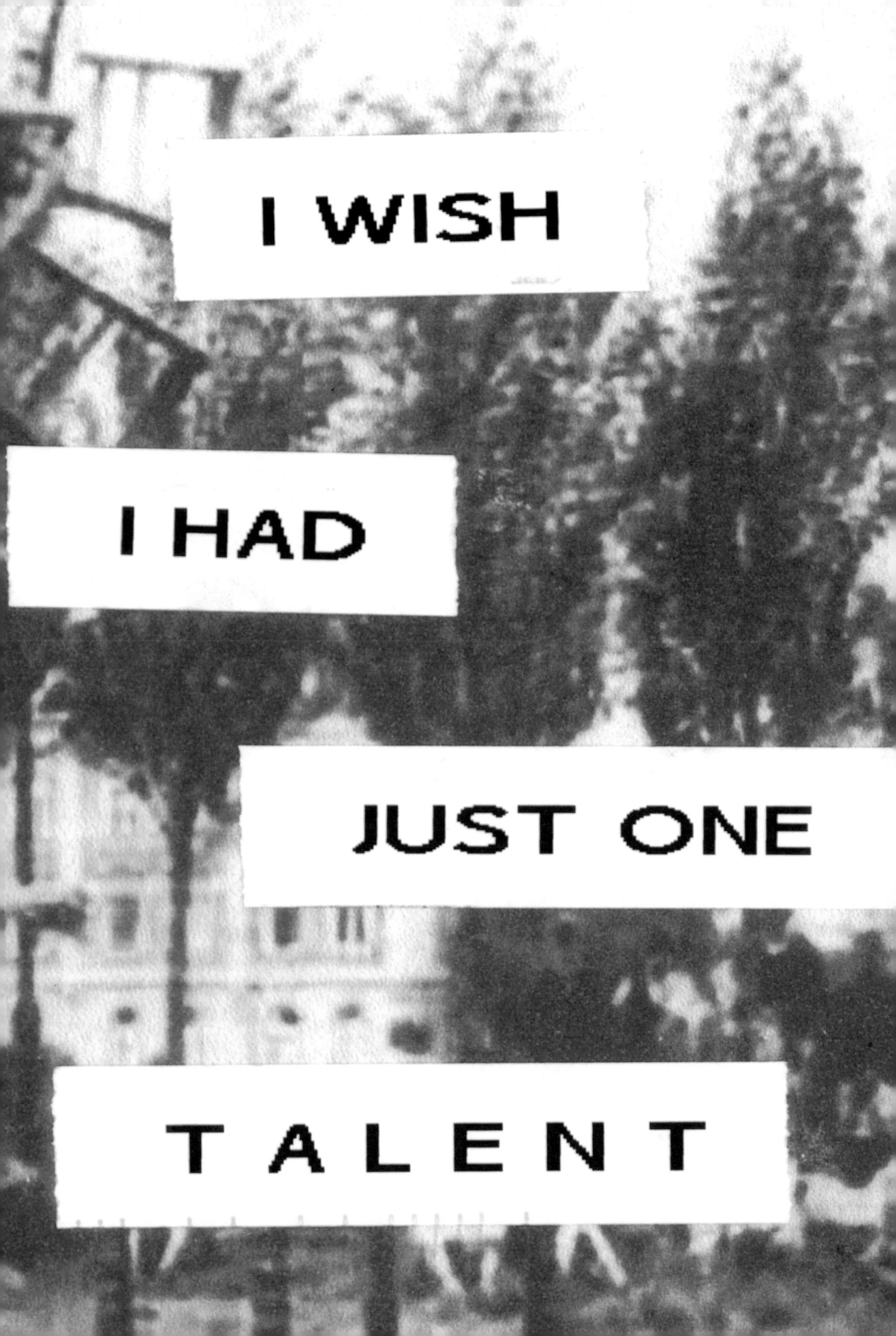
I WISH
I HAD
JUST ONE
TALENT

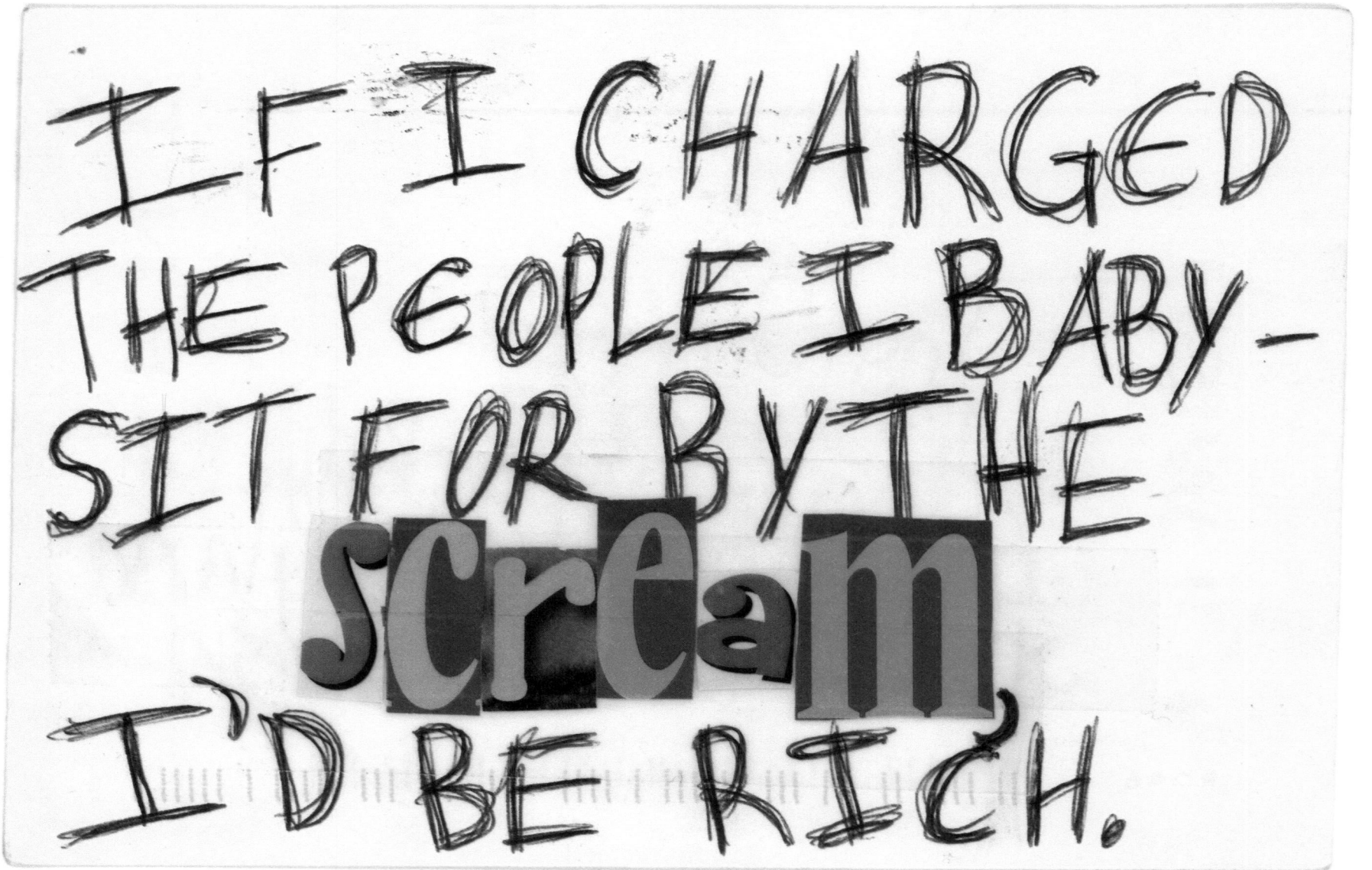
IF I CHARGED
THE PEOPLE I BABY-
SIT FOR BY THE
SCREAM
I'D BE RICH.

I'm only friend$ with
RICH girl$

Today, I masturbated in

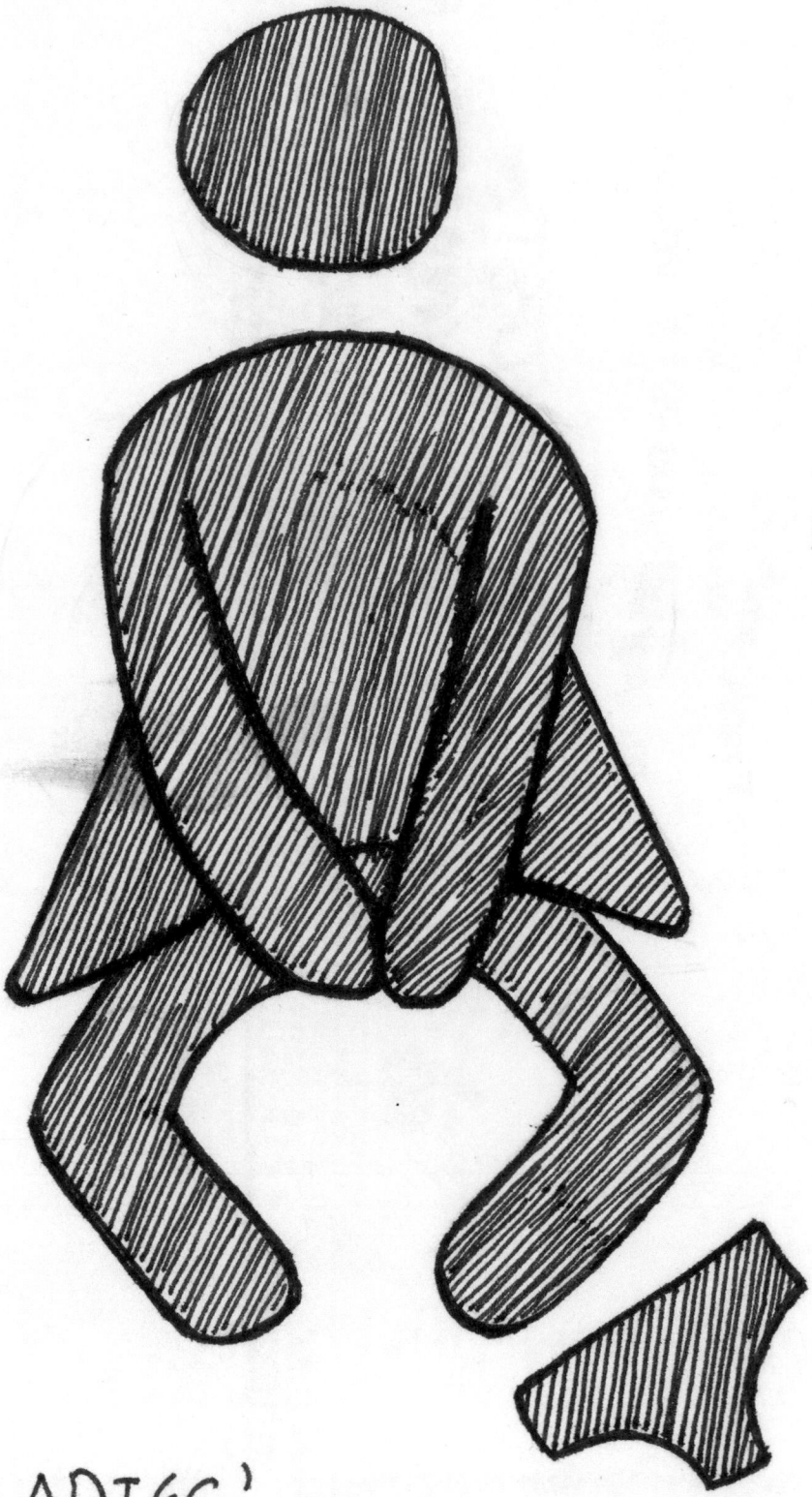

the LADIES' ROOM.

In elementary school, I started lying and telling everybody I was allergic to peanuts. This is my first peanut butter cup in years. I had to eat it in my car so my fiance wouldn't see. He thinks I'm allergic to them too.

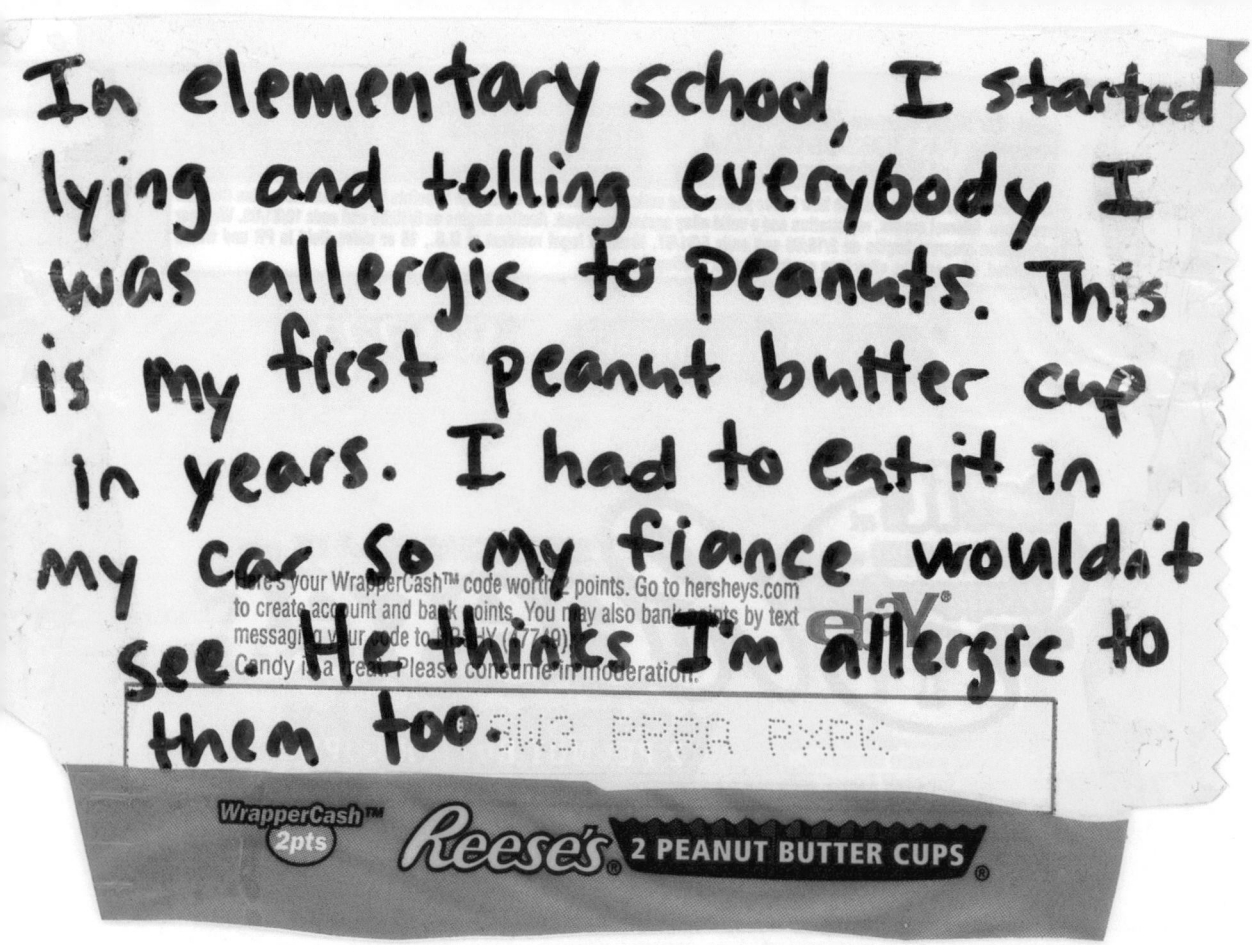

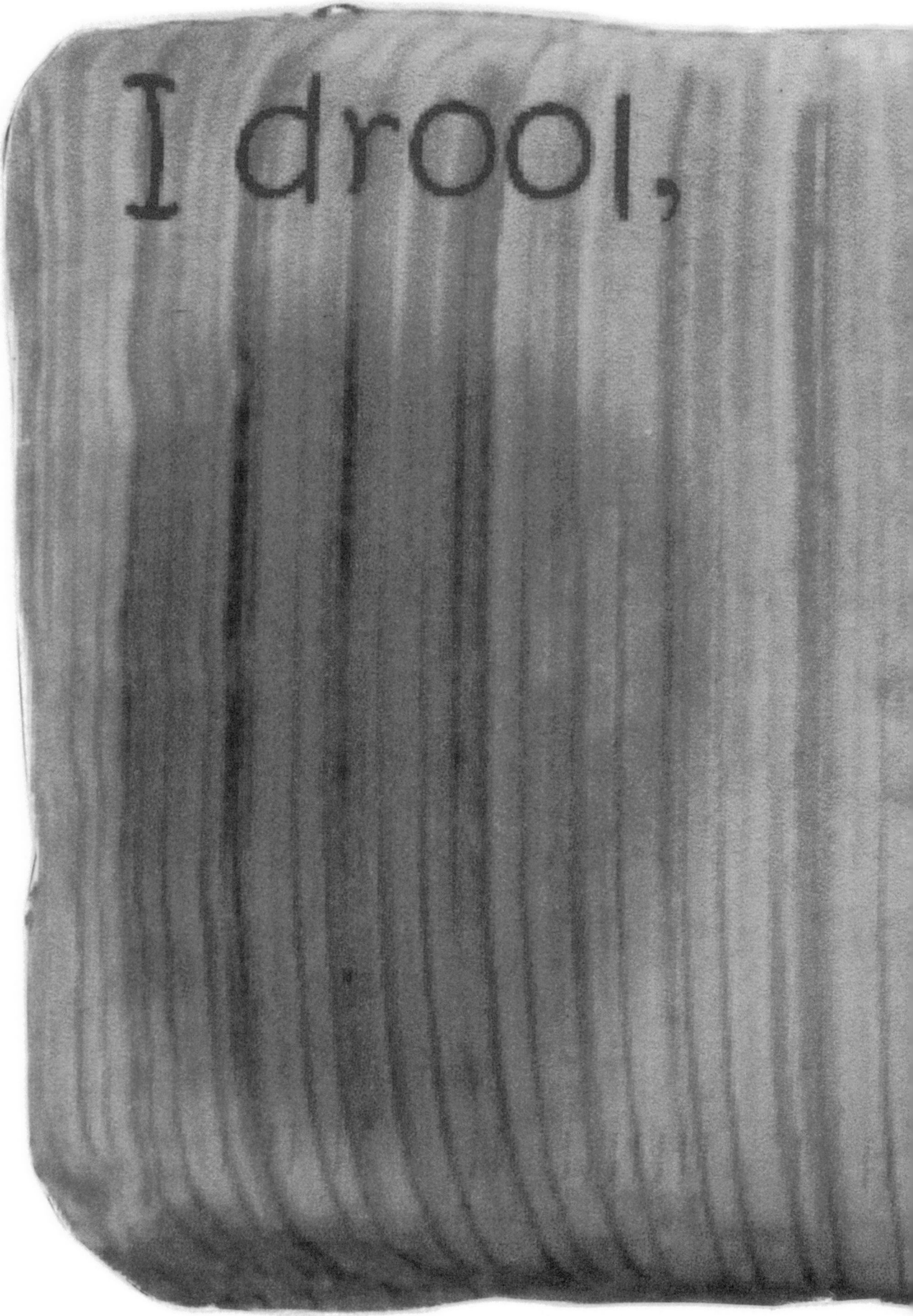
I drool,

a lot.

Although it's wonderful that you recommend 1(800) SUICIDE for suicidal people, not all people with secrets are depressed, oppressed, or scared. I think secrets are a good thing. It makes a person more mysterious, sexy, and unique. Secrets are fun, liberating; they make people who they are.

—Canada

AWKWARD
ENJOYABLE
CURIOUS
GROSS
BONDAGE
EXCELLENT
KINKY
I IMAGINE WHAT SEX WOULD BE LIKE WITH EVERY PERSON I INTERACT WITH.
PRUDE
MANLY
FUN
IMPOTENT
RAPE

I Lick the Inside of Microwave Popcorn Bags

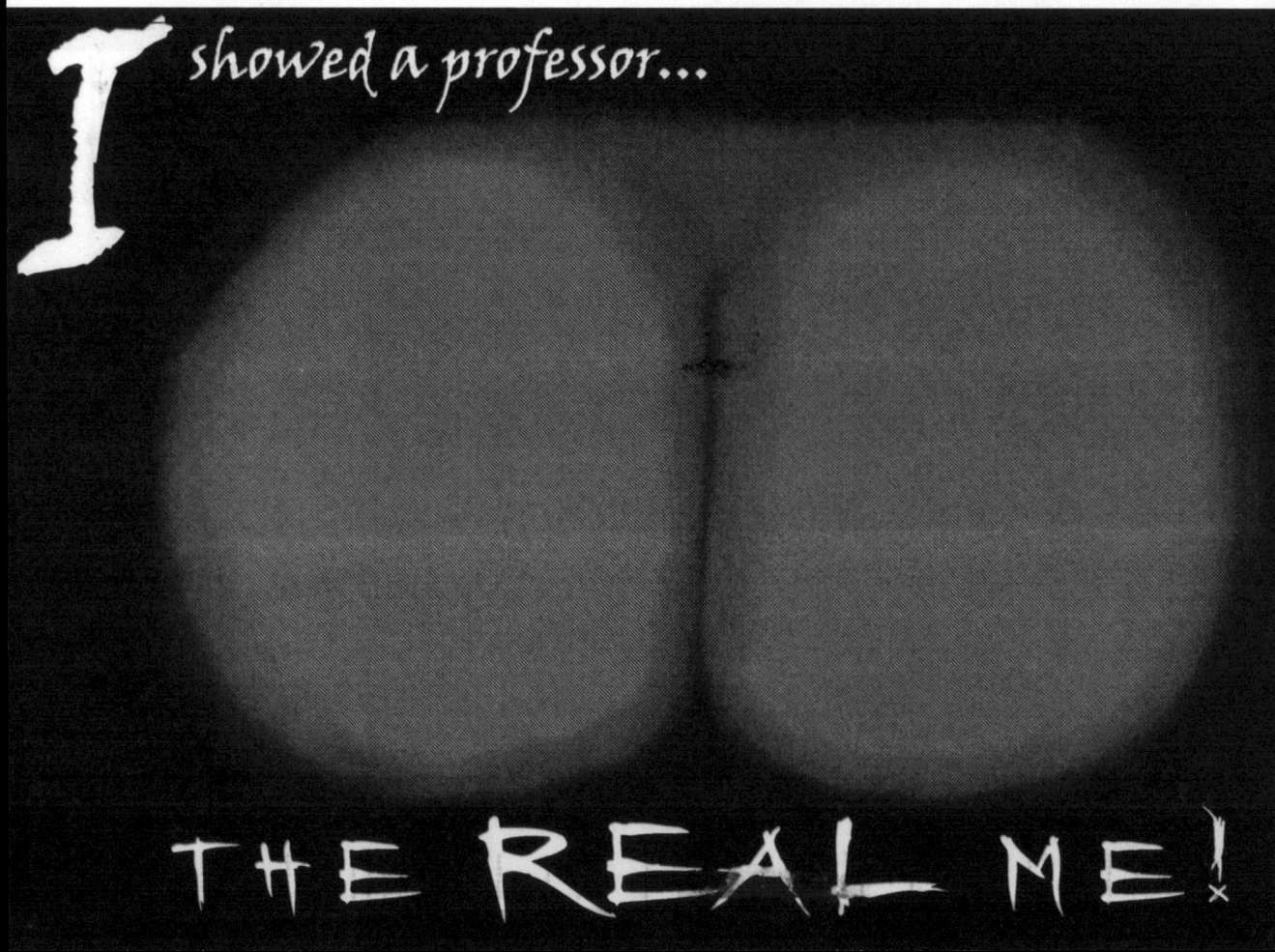

I'M ACheerleader;

but Secretly I deal drugs.

we watched my bipolar sister become a zombie on her meds.

I'm bipolar too

but I'm not seeking treatment

I like the highs and lows.....

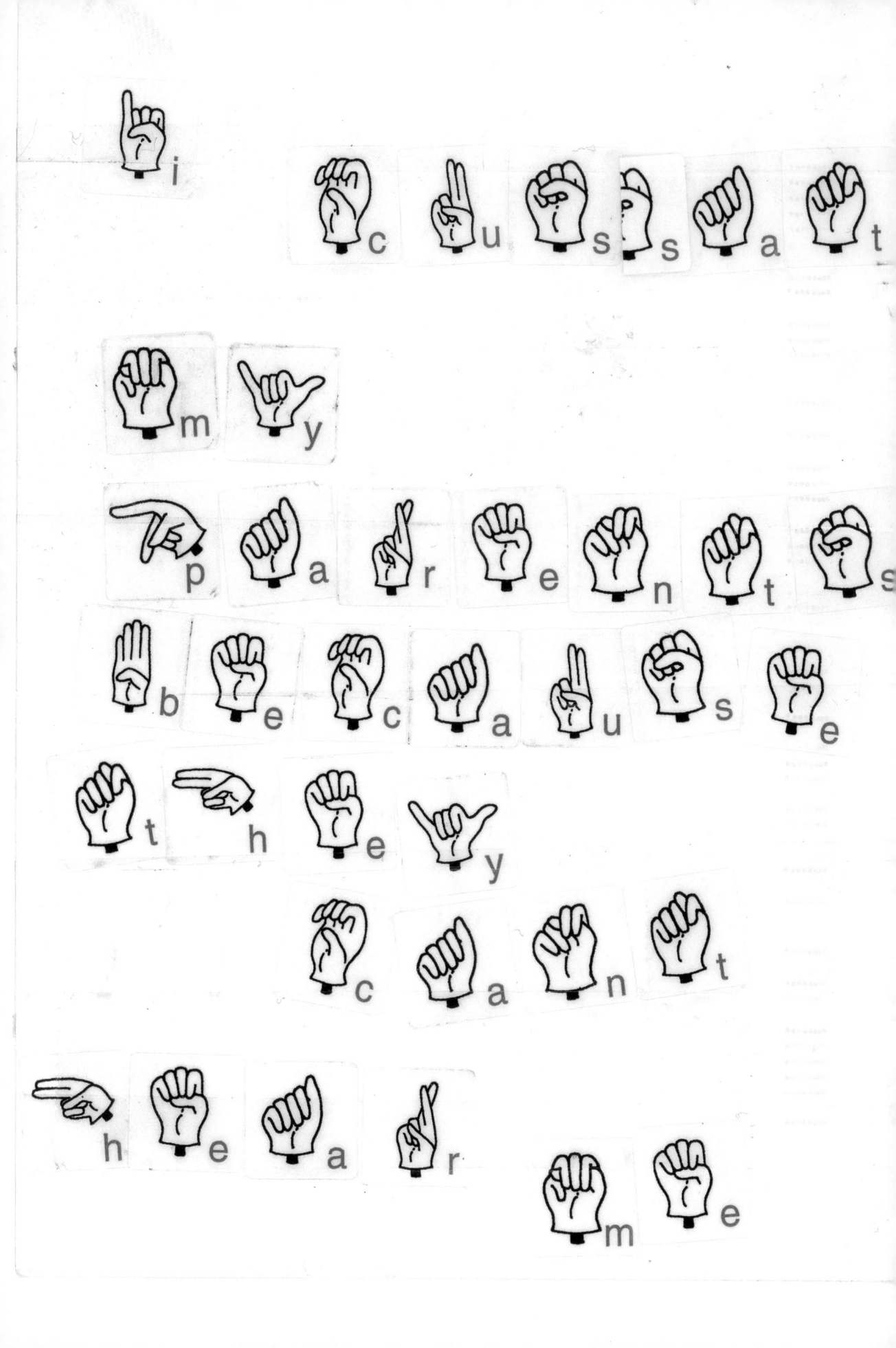
i
c u s s a t
m y
p a r e n t s
b e c a u s e
t h e y
c a n t
h e a r
m e

I was raped
on a beach.
I hate when ppl.
talk about sex
on the beach as
a sexy thing

I feel
out
of
place
in a
group
of
friends

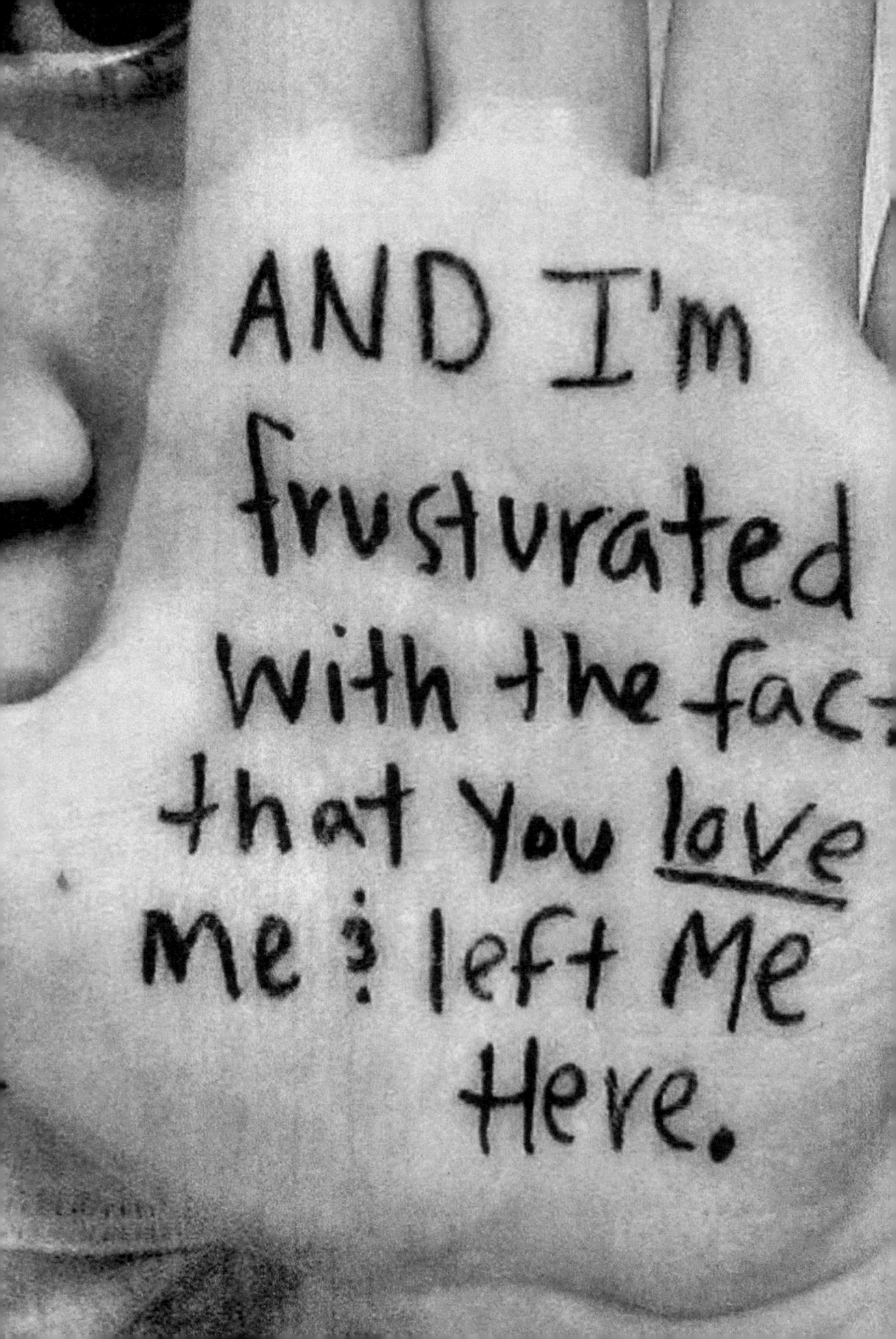
AND I'm
frustrated
with the fact
that you love
me ? left me
here.

I think I'd enjoy life on a deserted island because almost everybody gets on my nerves

I FORGOT TO PLAN WHAT HAPPENS NEXT

Popular Meter
Queen Bee
Me

I am avoiding you because you are socially below me.

You
Loser

When you were in the ICU
I took your picture.
I wanted you to see
what you looked like,
so that you might go into rehab.

I never showed you the pictures,
you never went into rehab,
and I never forgave myself

I am so sorry

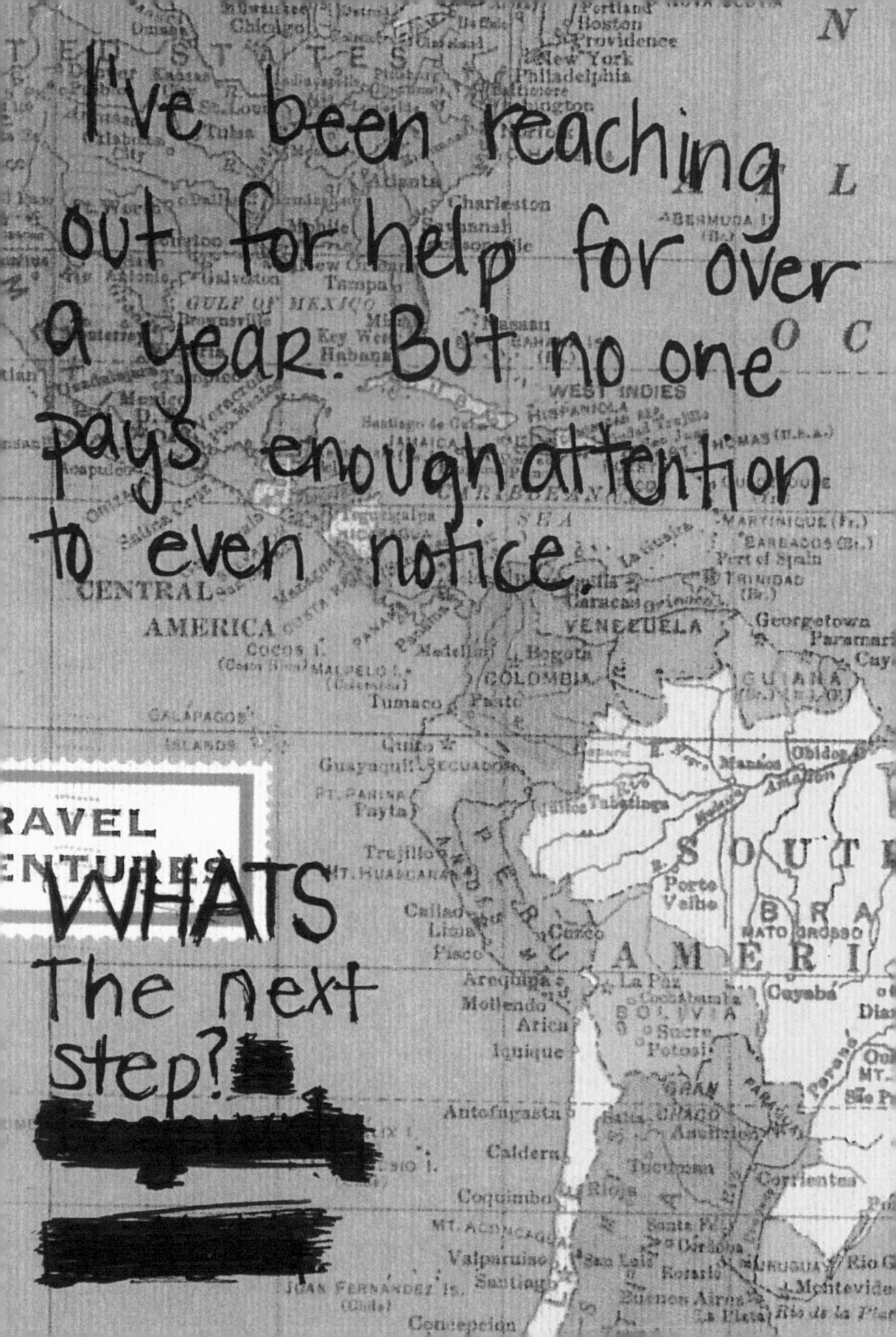
I've been reaching out for help for over a year. But no one pays enough attention to even notice.
RAVEL
ENTURES
WHATS
The next step?

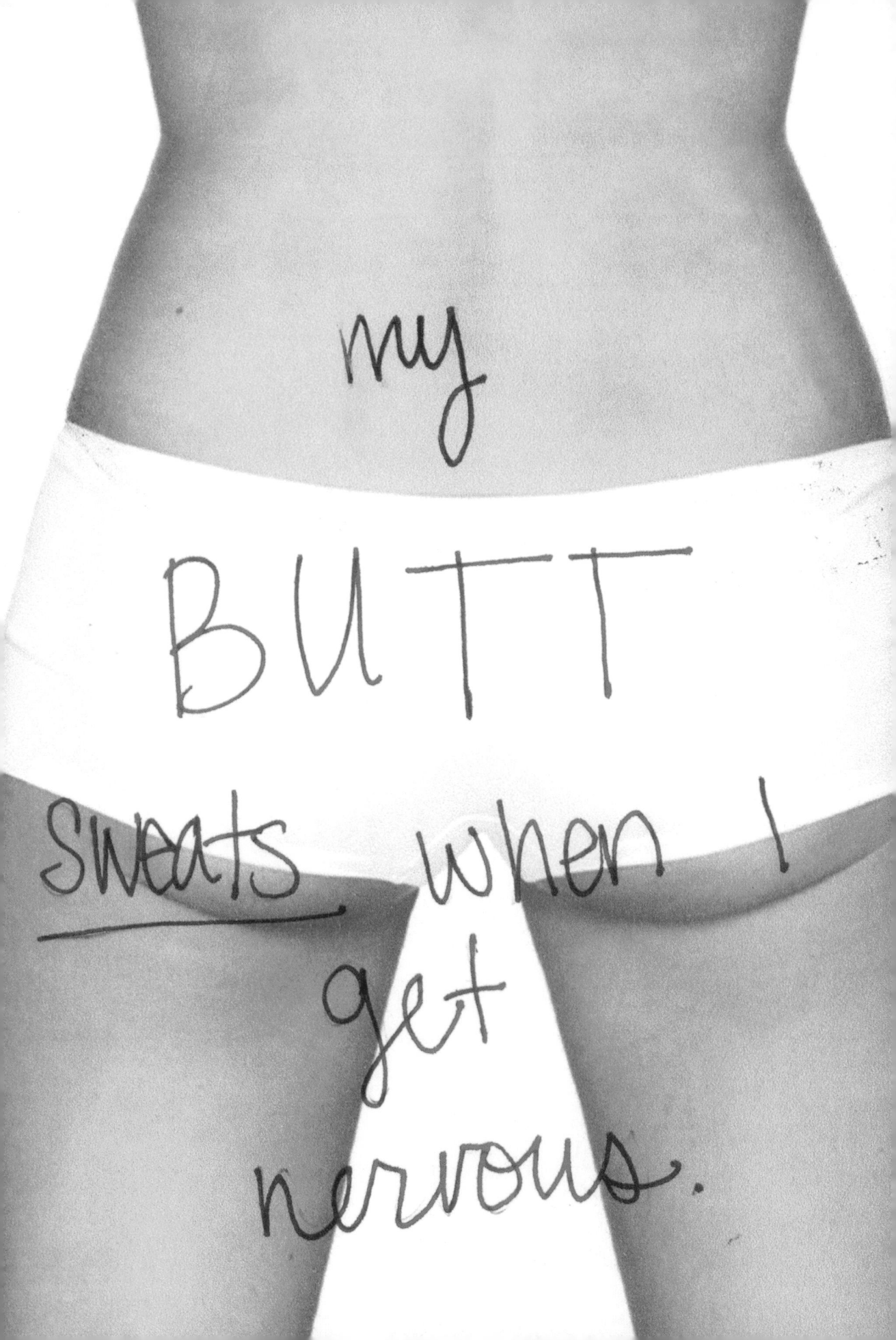
my
BUTT
sweats when I
get
nervous.

I have anger issues.

I know because

I often want

to kick the ass

of a total stranger

for no good reason.

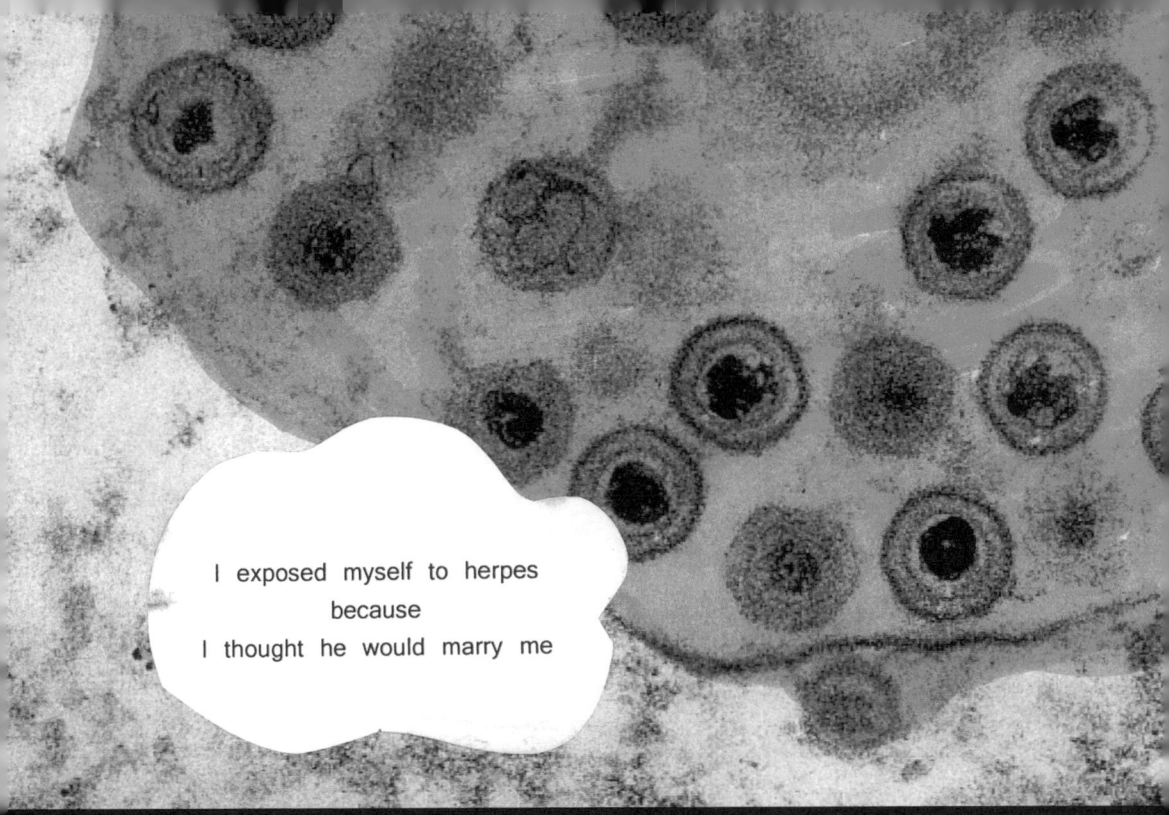

I WANT to
HAVE SEX
with a PIANO

I don’t feel entirely alone when I go through
still feel alone, but I feel like there are a lot

ne postcards on your website, or rather, I
nore people alone with me.

—New York

though i'm afraid you'll never speak to me again,

i'm pretty sure i'm better off that way.

interested in getti

for sure what you think o

to let you know that I like you a

nt me to, I'll try to stop because I don't

ying someone who doesn't like me. What's the message

And that's it. That's what I want to say. Did you mean

myself from ~~liking~~ doing it if there is no re

to like you. I've learned there is no point

Someone who does not like me back.

EITHERWAY, I'M KEEPING THE HAT.

MY
ANXIETY
IS OUT OF
CONTROL!!

I call my friend really late at night, secretly hoping she'll fall asleep while we're on the phone. Sometimes she does, and then I lie down to sleep too.
I'm in love with her and I realize it's probably the closest I'll ever get to sleeping with her.
But for now, it's enough.
Last call duration
06:54:04
Dialed calls' duration
38:14:50
Details
Back
metroPCS

I faked my own...
GRADUATION

My mom puts a star on the calendar for every day I haven't cut myself.

I don't deserve 5 of those stars...

Sorry.

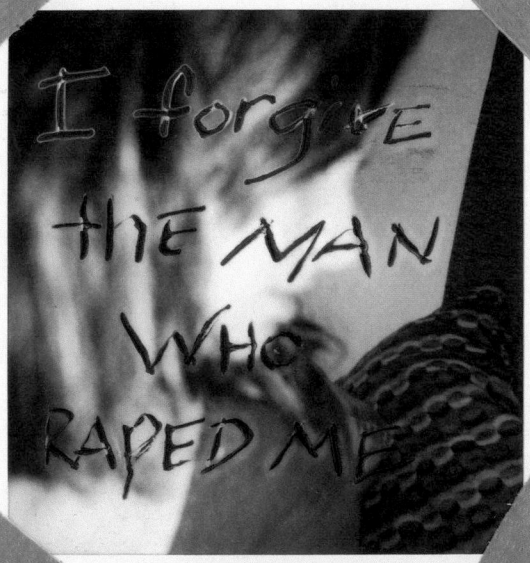

PostSecret
13345 Copper Ridge Rd
Germantown,
Maryland
20874-3454

Some days,
I don't mind
not being able
to go back
to who I was.

Tell him you're sorry but you can't. Open the door and go home.
I wish the DIVINE HAD INTERVENED

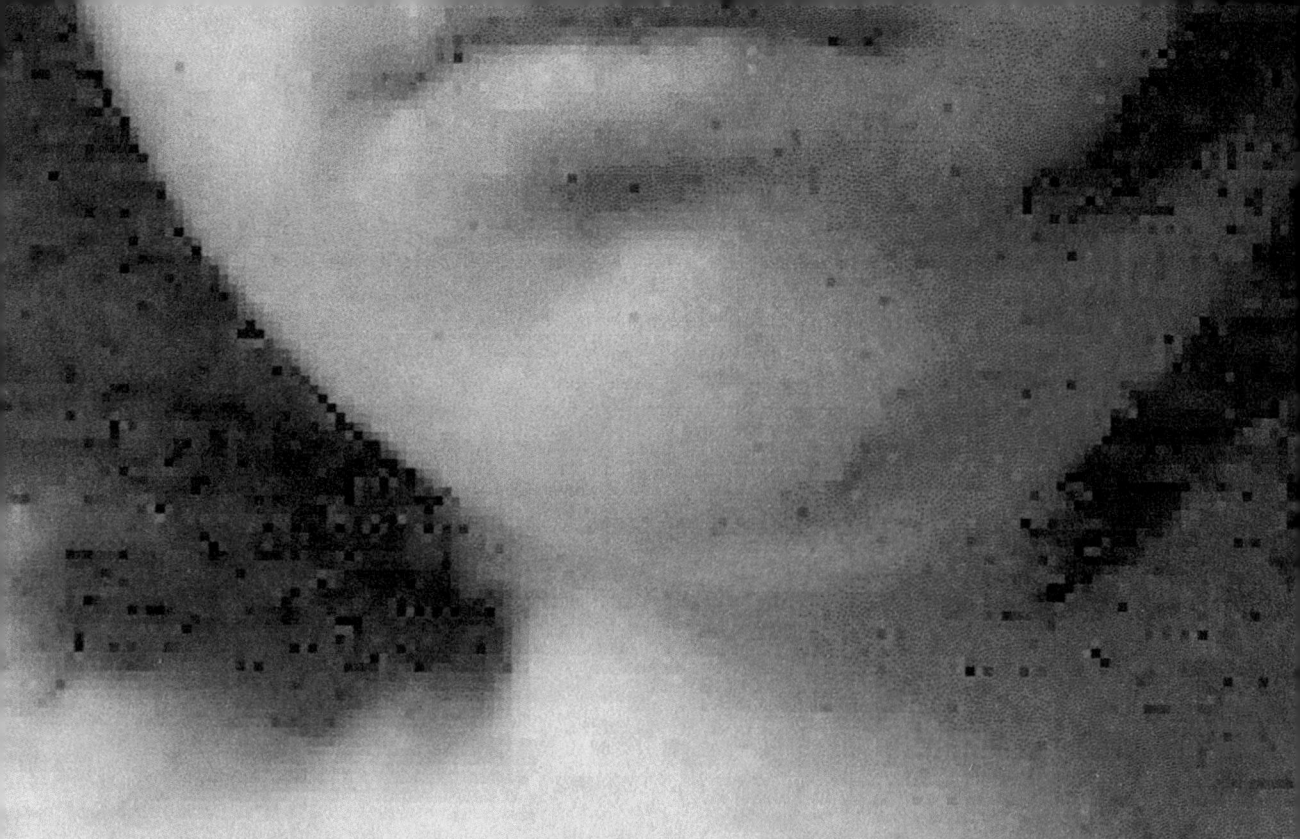

everyday I worry
my exboyfriend
will use the naked
pictures I sent him
to ruin my life

I

TOLD

MYFAMILY

THESCHOOLNURSE

ANDMYOPTOMETRIST

THATICOULDNTSEETHELASTROWS

JUSTSOTHATIWOULDGETGLASSESLIKEMYFRIENDS

in the 3rd grade, a boy told me i looked like
a werewolf because my arms were so hairy.
for the rest of the year, i wore long-sleeved
shirts and turtlenecks. even in the summer.
now i just shave my arms.

i wonder if he remembers.

MY FAVOURITE PART ABOUT WORKING AT LEGO LAND IS DESTROYING ALL OF THE BUILDINGS THAT LITTLE KIDS CREATE

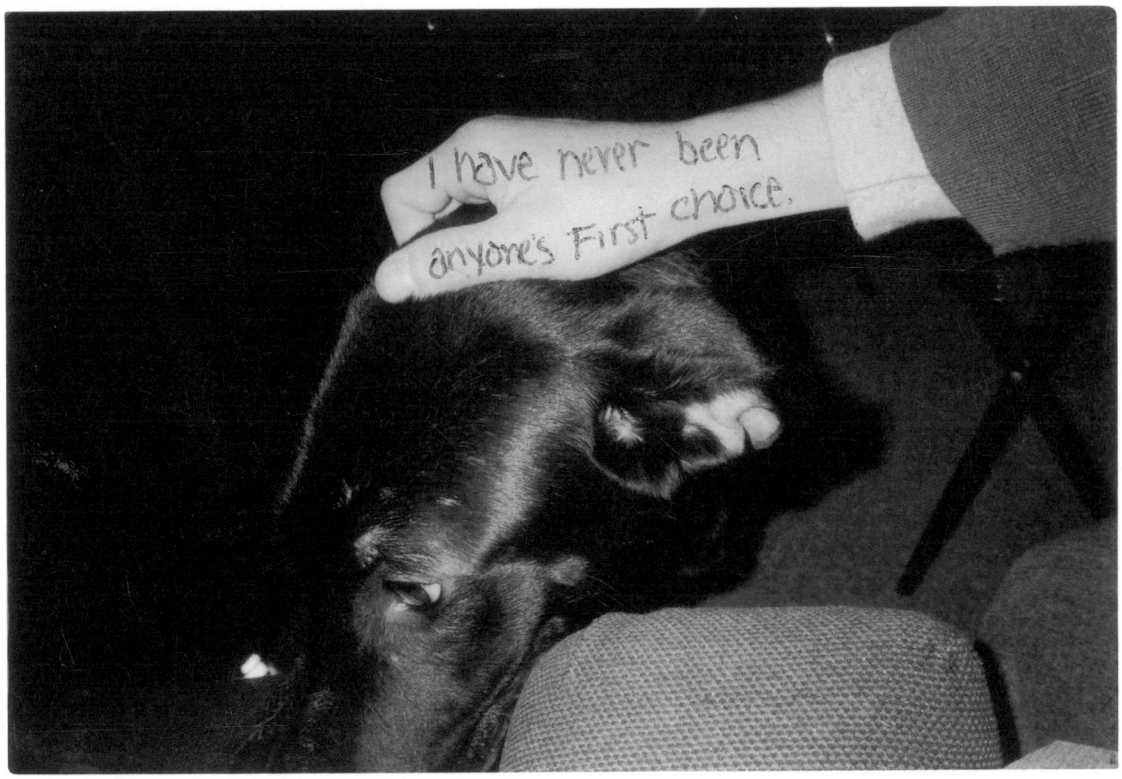

Every regret I've ever had involved alcohol.

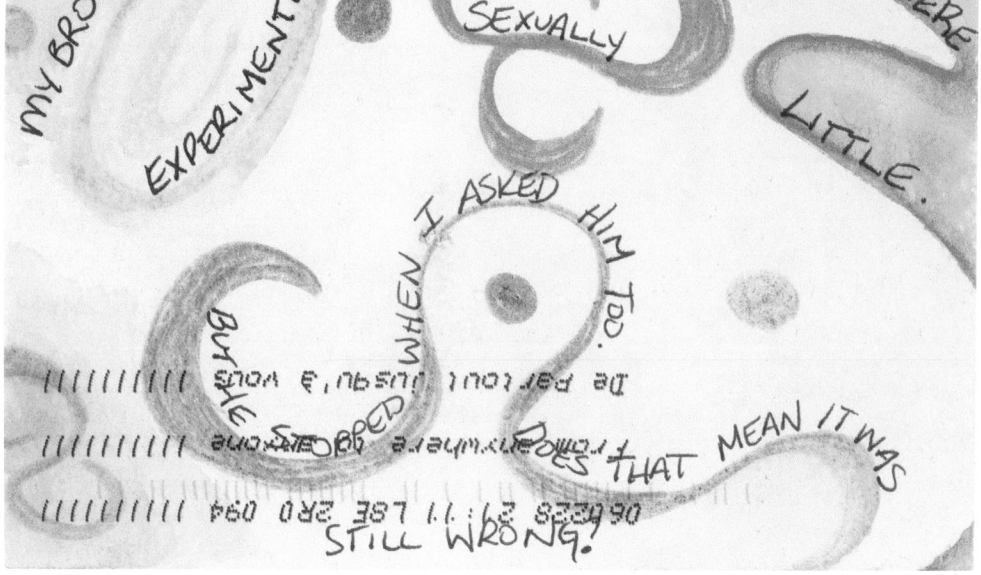

i know you didn't rape me

but i convinced myself that you did
because i was unwilling to admit
that i lost my virginity to you.

when i write in my journal, i feel like im writing a novel about a stranger; "one girl's demise to insanity"

[redacted]

HE SAID HE DIDN'T
LIKE CONDOMS
SO WE DIDN'T USE ONE...
BUT I DIDN'T TELL HIM
I HAVE HERPES.....

TROJAN

POSTSECRET

13345 COPPER RIDGE RD

GERMANTOWN, MARYLAND

20874-3454

GO CARD® Nationwide Postcard Advertising ☎ 212.925.2420

EVERY DAY I PRAY THAT YOU WILL STAND UP

SAVE ME NO MATTER WHAT I'LL DO YOU

AT MY WEDDING WHEN THE PRIEST ASKS IF ANYONE HAS A REASON THESE TWO SHALL NOT WED.

I LOVE YOU

I DON'T WANT TO BE HERE ANYMORE

I AM COUNTING ON YOU.

I can stop playing anytime I want.

Barely Here.

I'm extra nice to blacks to show them that I am nothing like my forefathers.

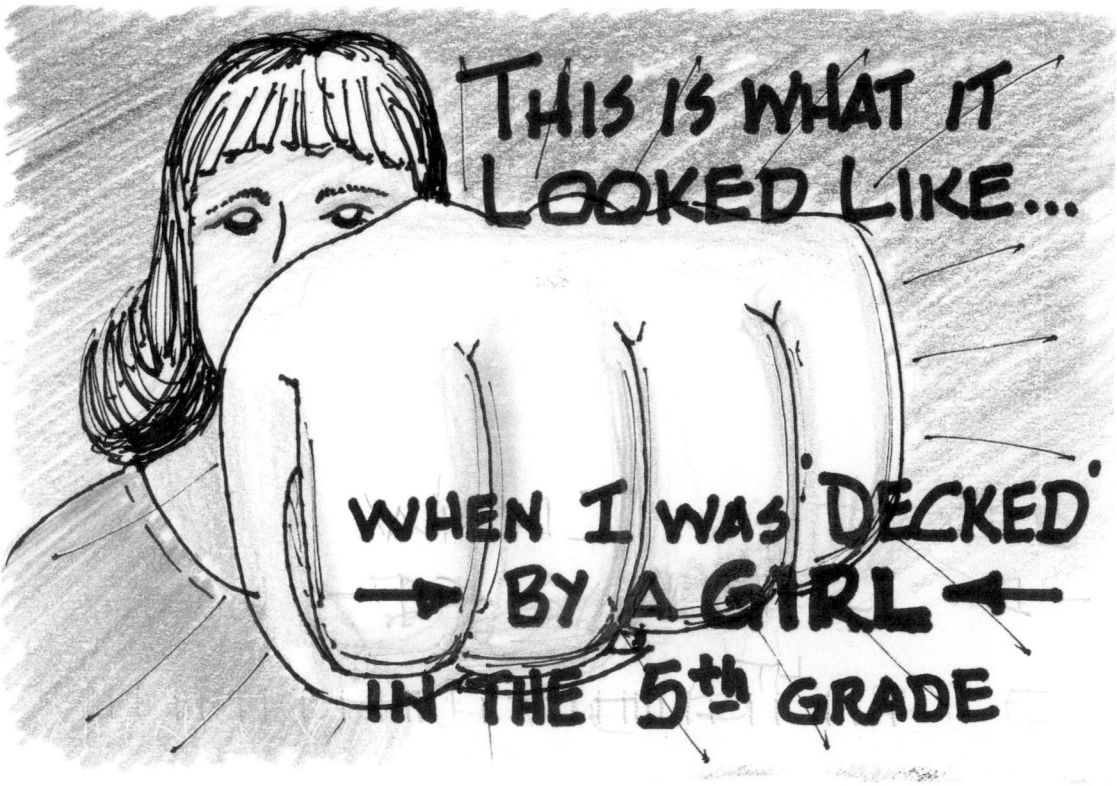
THIS IS WHAT IT LOOKED LIKE...
WHEN I WAS DECKED BY A GIRL IN THE 5th GRADE

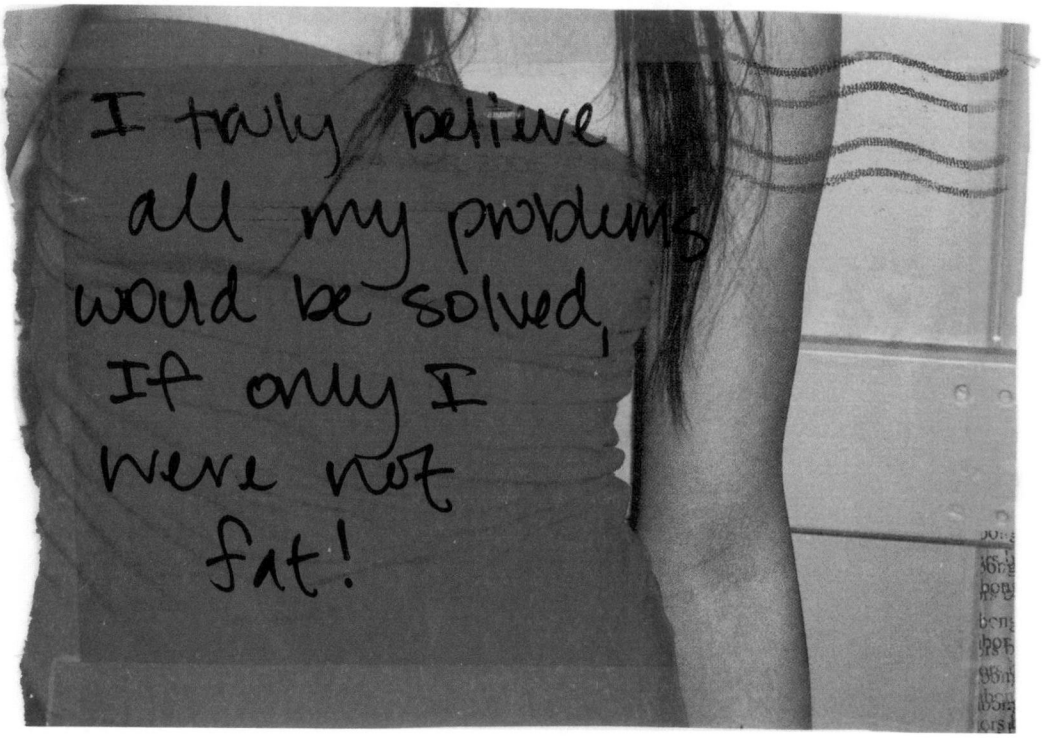
I truly believe all my problems would be solved, If only I were not fat!

I've been trying to be you
that I forgot what it's like

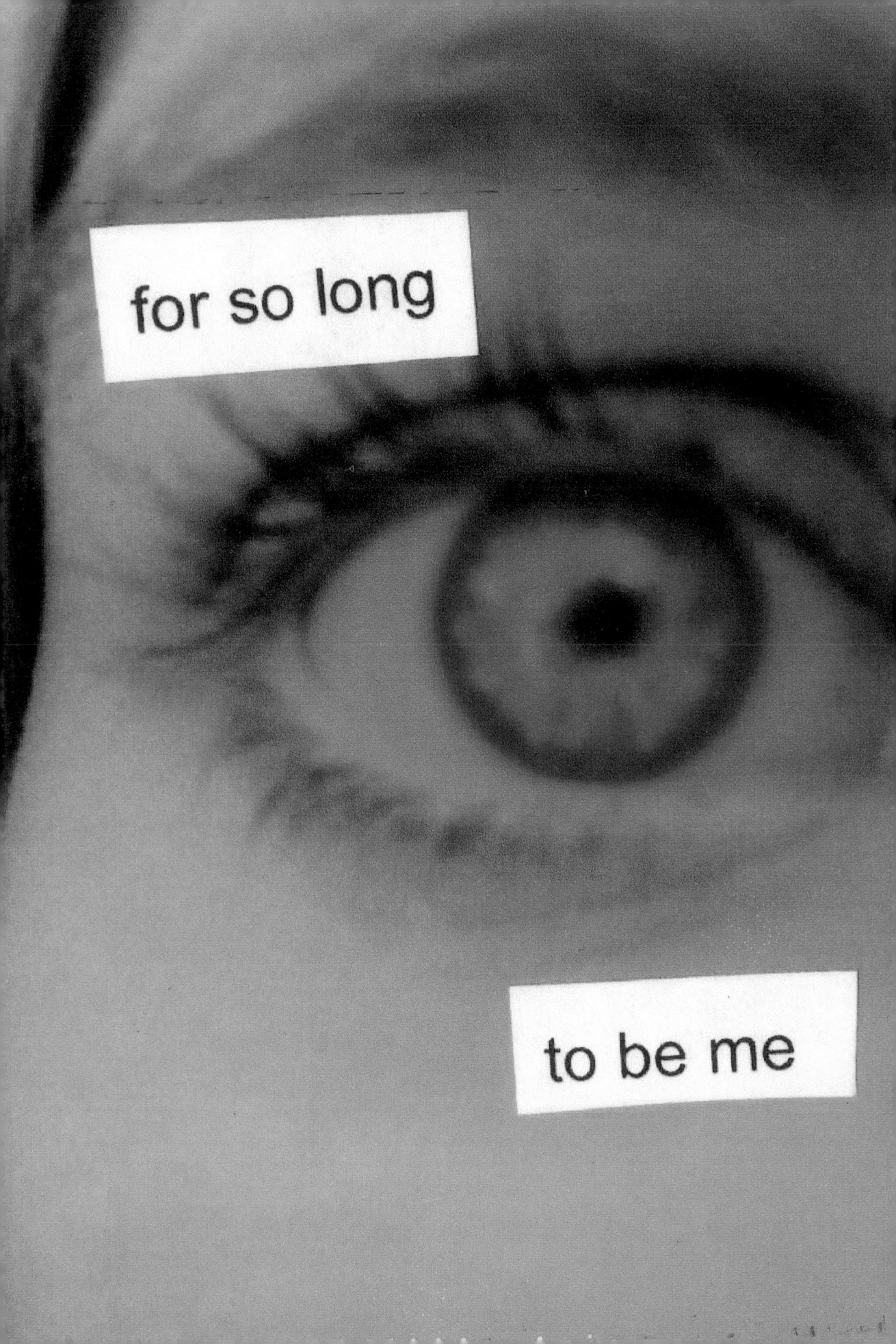
for so long
to be me

I can't wait
till I prove
them all wrong.

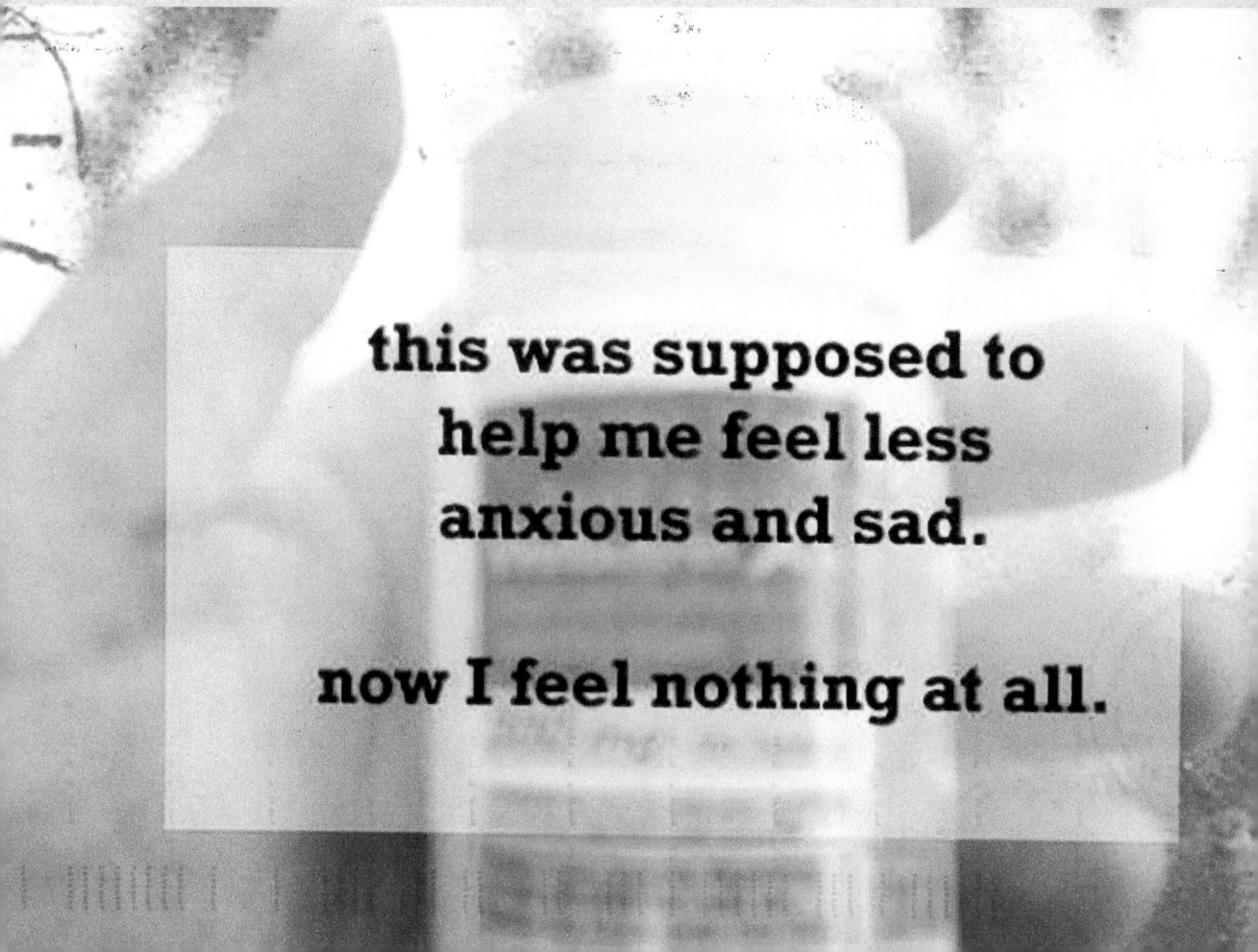

I Can't Stand my Roommate.

I cheated my way through

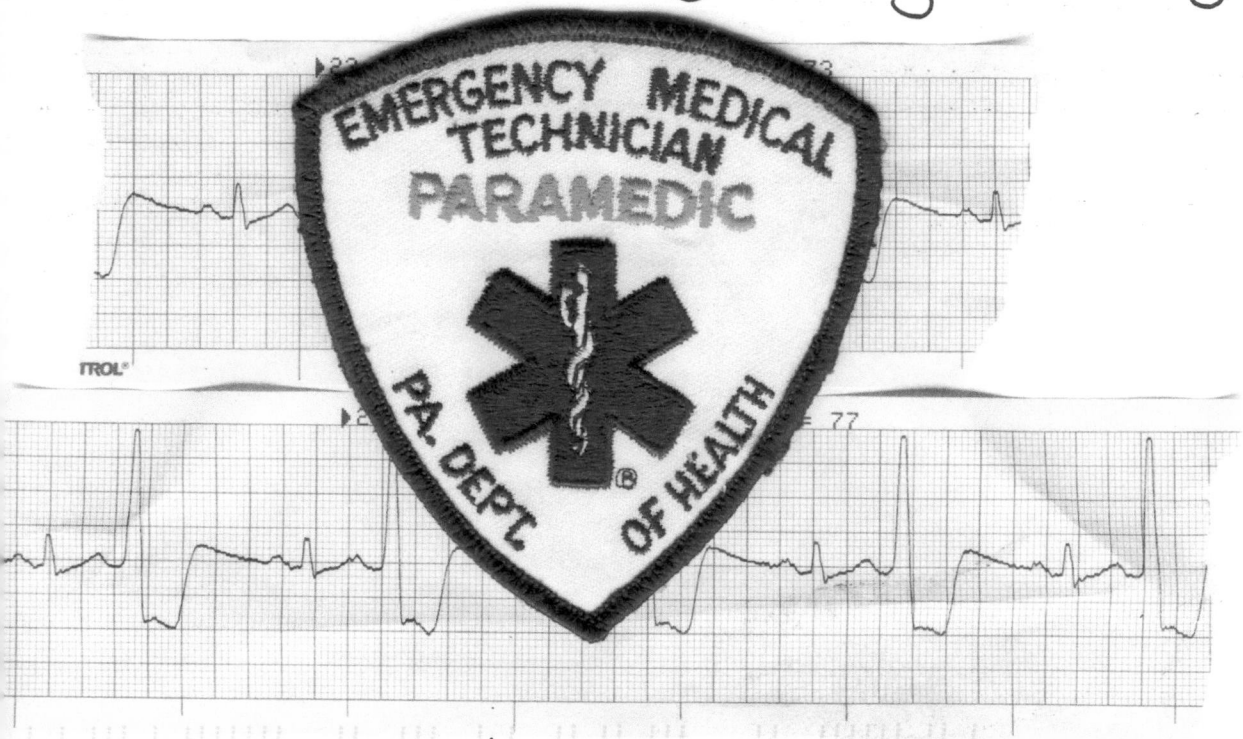

school.

I still look at your 3rd grade picture and think what might have happened...

If I hadn't moved 825 miles away

THE CATCHER IN THE RYE

J.D. SALINGER

If you feel like you are going insane, and you are trapped in a dysfunctional environment, You Are Not Crazy.

DEEP DOWN
I'VE ALWAYS BELIEVED
I AM MEANT FOR SOMETHING
REALLY BIG...
NOW
I'M JUST WAITING.

I KNOW THE
TRUTH TO THE
LIE MY
PARENTS
TELL...
But they don't know I do.

¡CANONLY
LOVEHER
WHENSHE
LEAVESME

FIRST CLASS
USA
2006
- POST SECRET -
13345 Copper Ridge Rd.
GERMANTOWN, MD.
20874

For Better	For Worse
He tries to make me happy • He likes to keep the apartment clean • He's great in bed--we really have great sex together • I love it when we cuddle • He teases me in a fun way • I like waking up next to him • I enjoy feeling him inside me • His happiness makes me happy • He doesn't like me to swear or yell at him • He helps me avoid mistakes • He says I turn him on • I like to think of ways to make him happier • My family likes him a lot and thinks he is good person for me to be with • He asked me if I want to get married	He frustrates me • I do most of the cleaning while he relaxes • He's not interested in sex most of the time • He develops various pains when we cuddle • I can't tease back • He's very grumpy when he wakes up • He'd rather jack-off • He is easily offended or angered • He swears and yells at me • He critiques almost everything I do • Other people turn him on a lot more • He doesn't think of me most of the time • I don't tell them any of this because I don't want them to think negatively of him • I'm not sure if I do, but I said yes.

I sleep to escape

My grandmother
used to mail me
26 MAY 2006 PM 2
postcards like this
(blank ones) so I
would write to her.
She died seven years ago, and I
just found this one in the attic.
I'm sorry, Grandma.

© USPS 1995

... I should have written more

Sometimes I

WiSH

I was better

at faking

it.

Sometimes when we think we are keeping

a secret, that secret is actually keeping us.

—Frank

Inside this envelope are the scraps of my old life.
But I realized... I don't need this anymore, I'm alive
again. Everything is okay. My soul has been reborn +
I couldn't be more happy!

And let me tell you....
there is nothing more invigorating or life-affirming
then shredding old suicide notes.

I SAW YOUR SECRET...

POSTAGE DUE 2

POST SECRET
13345 COPPER RIDGE RD
GERMANTOWN, MARYLAND
20874

R045

AND I LOVE YOU ANYWAY.

MY HEART IS AN
IDIOT

I Am Afraid That the
Only Thing I like to Do, won't
TAKE me anywhere.
I hope I am wrong.
sometimes...
i miss God.

I was molested for most of my childhood.

Sometimes I liked it.

I will always hate myself for that.

I told my mom I was going to a friend's house when I was really going to a
hotel with my best friends to get drunk for the first time.

I hate
highschool
because it has made
my best relationships
go up in smoke.

I am afraid to live
a Christian life
because I might
miss out
on all the fun

When do we tell them

there will be TWO brides on the cake?

When I masturbate, the first thought that pops into my head after I climax is
"OK, what was the point of that?"

I lie to my mother about my finances so she won't worry about me. She thinks my bills are paid. In reality I am in debt $85000.

I LIED, MOM.
I WAS HIGH
WHEN I DREW
DOUG ON MY
FOOT.

I will always be the weird
quiet girl.

Purple line to Linden
I want to tell you that I understand what you are telling me more and more every day, and I wish I could be more open with you.
The best secrets I ever kept...
were hers.

It's always been my dream to attend Harvard Law School.

Now that I'm here, I'm counting down the days until I can leave

Then I remembered myself.

Enjoy your new important life and f*@k you.

You were the only one I thought I could count on.

(I was molested)

There, I said it

I desperately want someone
to recognize one of my
secrets so I can finally
stop pretending

What YOU!
did will not
Define ME!
I Broke FREE!

I work with a lot of old people and
they
drive me nuts
Sneezer's
SNACK SHOP

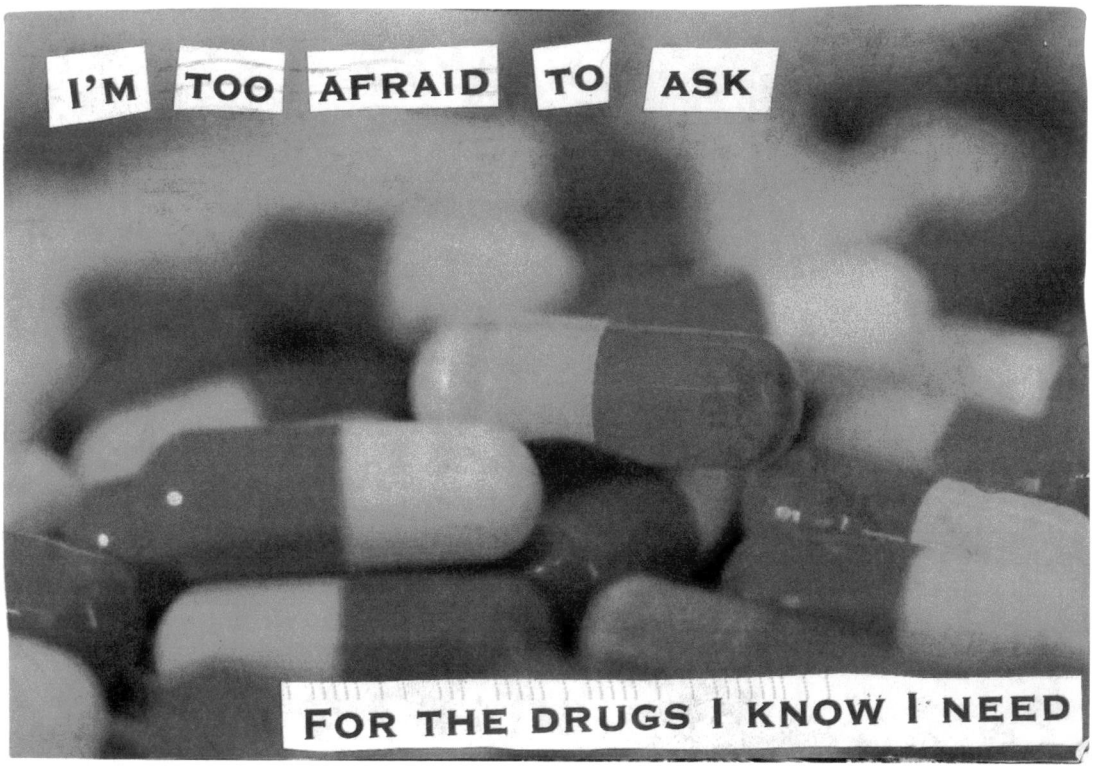
I'M TOO AFRAID TO ASK
FOR THE DRUGS I KNOW I NEED

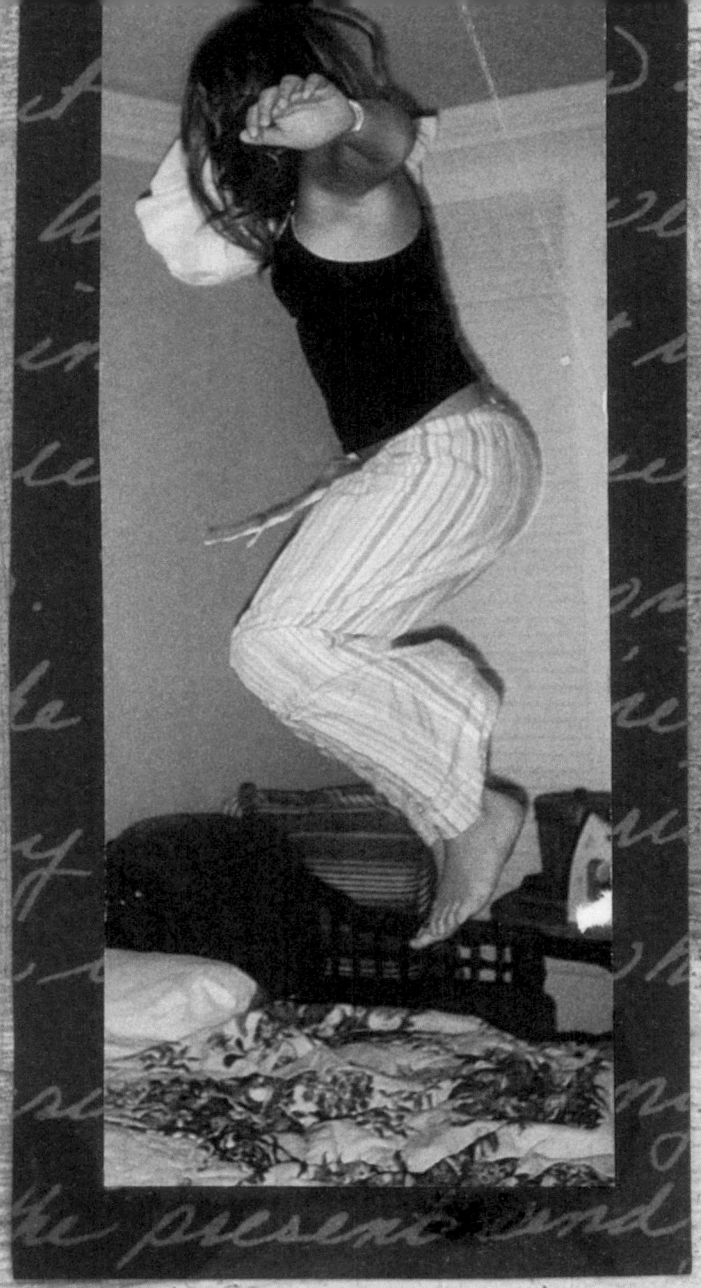

I don't remember when jumping on the bed stopped being fun... but I dream of returning to such carefree days...

DAD, I KNOW YOU KEEP
YOUR GUN LOADED
AND UNLOCKED

I orgasm when I swim laps.
(Only once and usually around the 400 meter mark.)

I WAS A BITCH
TO YOU
I KNEW YOU LOVED ME
I'M SO SORRY

I don't believe that "perfect families" exist...
They all fuck you up...

i sometimes wish no one told me i was adoqted

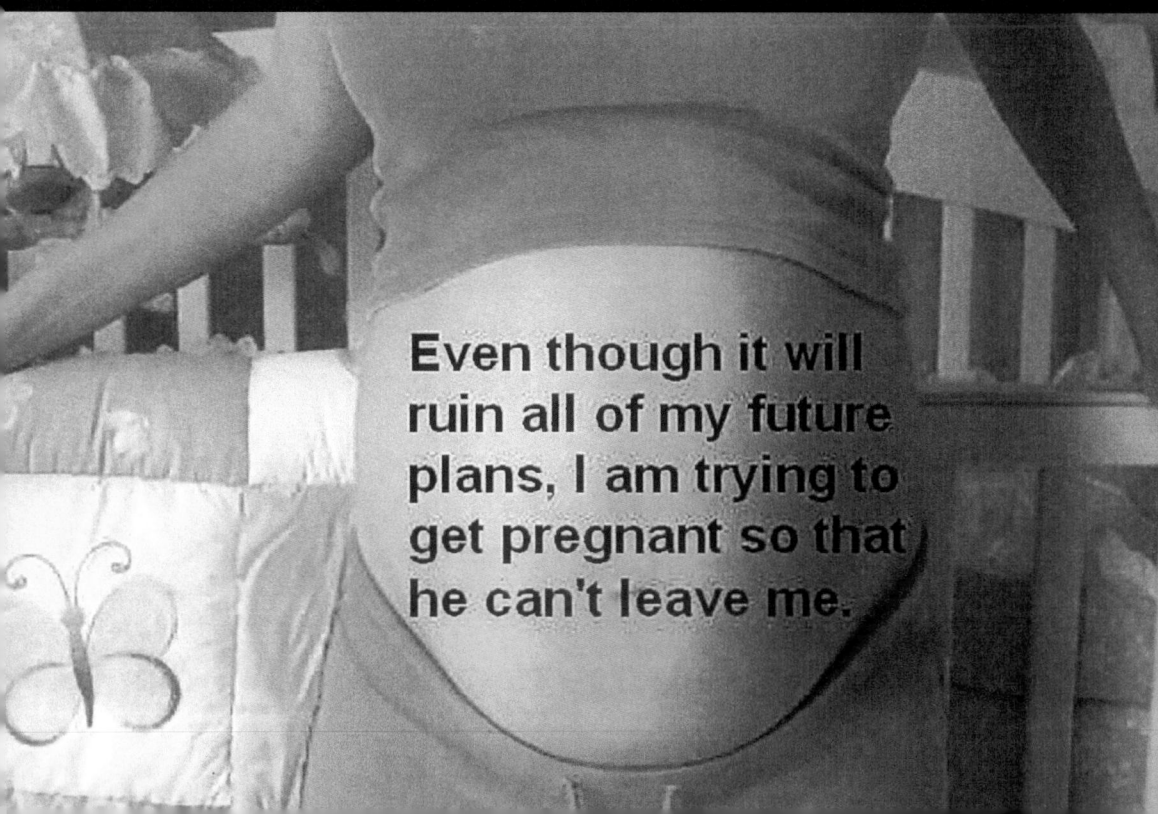

1
2
3
7
8
9
13
14
15

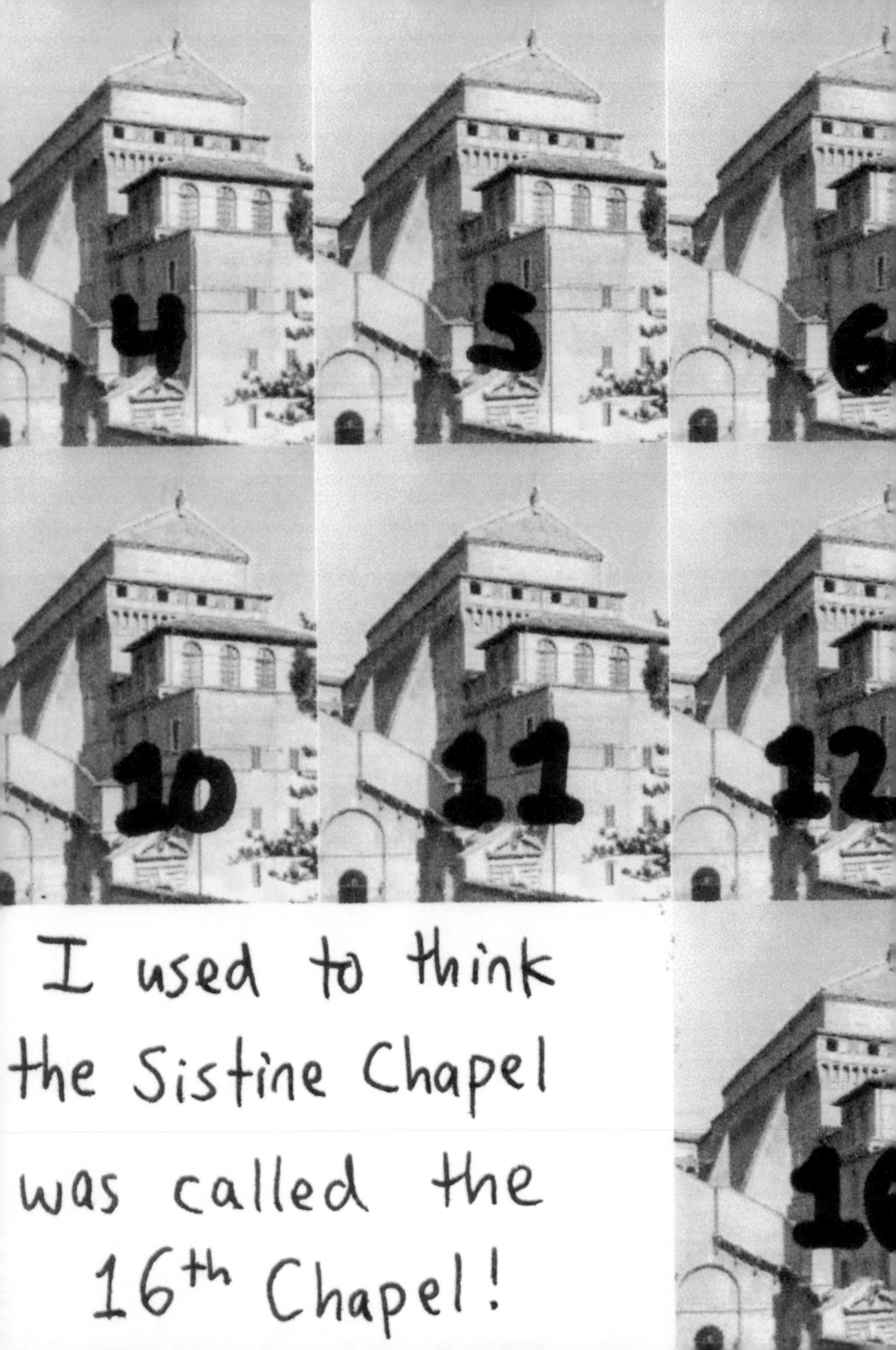

I used to think
the Sistine Chapel
was called the
16th Chapel!

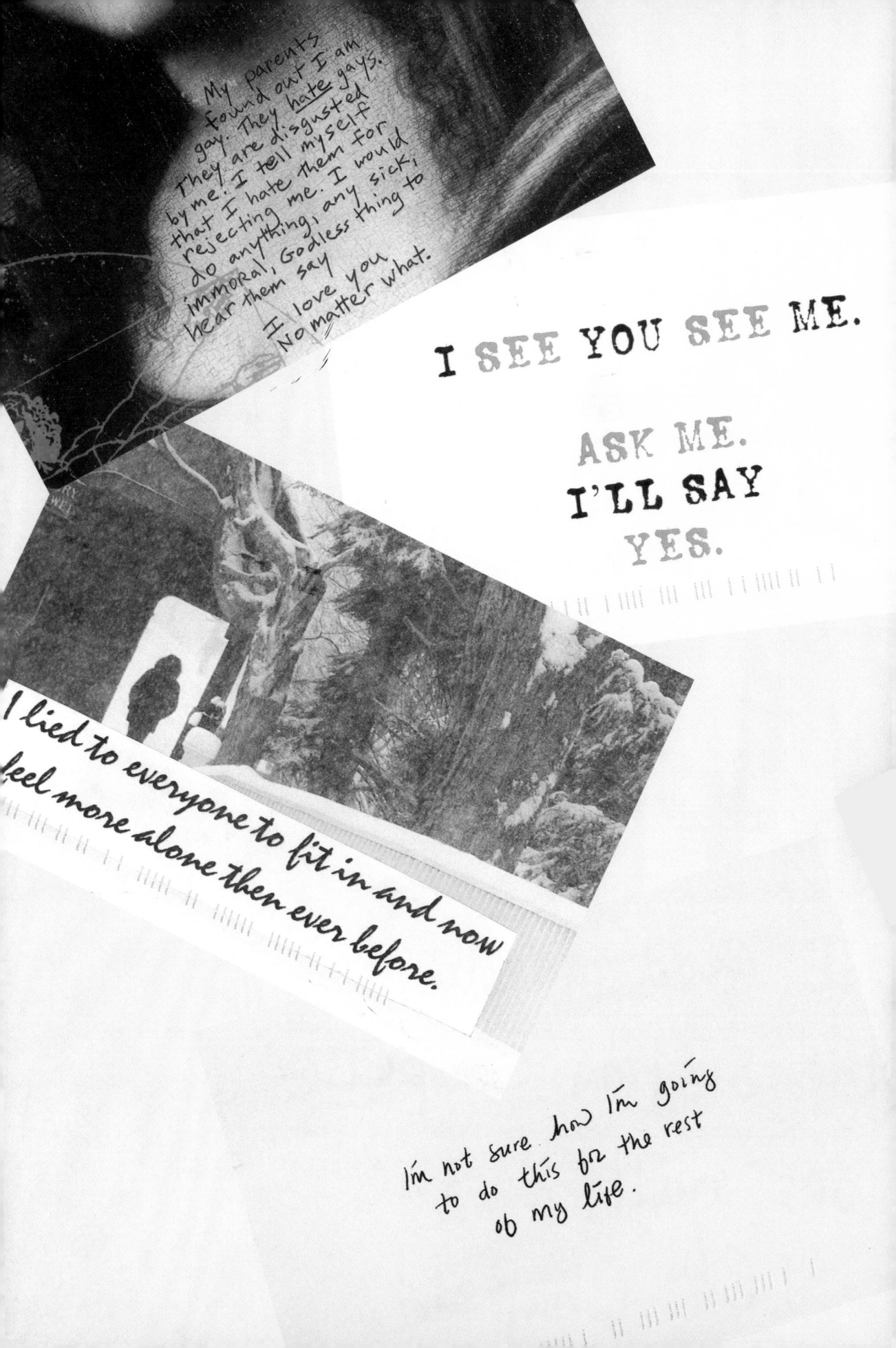
My parents found out I am gay. They hate gays. They are disgusted by me. I tell myself that I hate them for rejecting me. I would do anything, any sick, immoral, Godless thing to hear them say
I love you
No matter what.
I SEE YOU SEE ME.
ASK ME.
I'LL SAY
YES.
I lied to everyone to fit in and now feel more alone then ever before.
I'm not sure how I'm going to do this for the rest of my life.

Anorexia ate my
SOUL
I'm not as smart as I lead on.
THIS IS ME BEFORE I REACH THE
POINT OF NO RETURN.
I don't
know
how to
say
NO

I'm Scared
I'll always
Go into
Photobooths alone

I am terrified
of growing up.

In 6th grade I read something about,
father's molesting their daughters.
So, I stopped hugging my dad
for over a year.
I love my father.
I can't imagine how much
I hurt him.

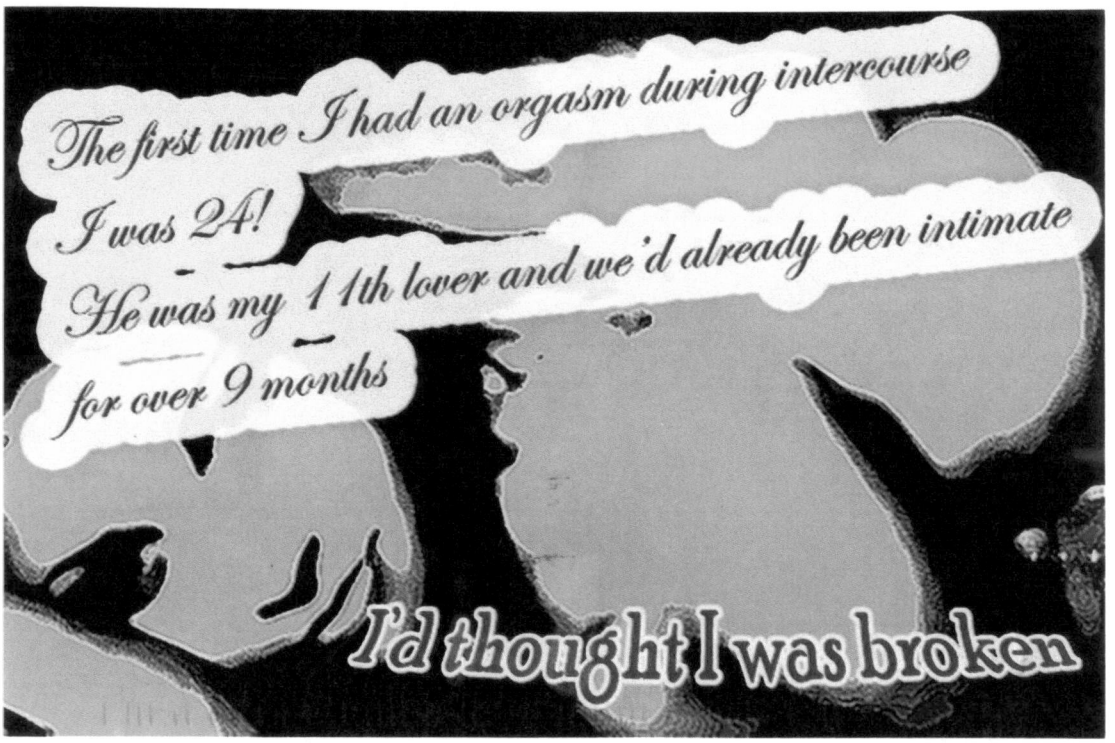
The first time I had an orgasm during intercourse
I was 24!
He was my 11th lover and we'd already been intimate
for over 9 months
I'd thought I was broken

EVERYONE THINKS I WANT TO CHANGE THE WORLD...
...REALLY, I JUST WANT A COMFORTABLE LIFE.
(BUT I'M ASHAMED TO ADMIT THAT)

I like it when you sing
Because it makes me feel better about my voice.

Post Secret
13345 Copper Ridge L
Germantown, MD
20874-3454

I CUT MY HAIR
OFF CUS MY
PARENTS
love
their SALON more
THAN
ME

I just want
to be a
good
person.

I'm starting to realize that all my problems can't be blamed on anything else but myself – only I can make my life what I want it to be and everyday my self-control and self-discipline fuck it up more and more.

I miss the days when I thought there was something wrong with me.

I'M SORRY MOM,
I'M SPENDING YOUR
MONEY ON THINGS
THAT ARE KILLING ME

I am afraid that since my Dad is

GAY

that I might be too.

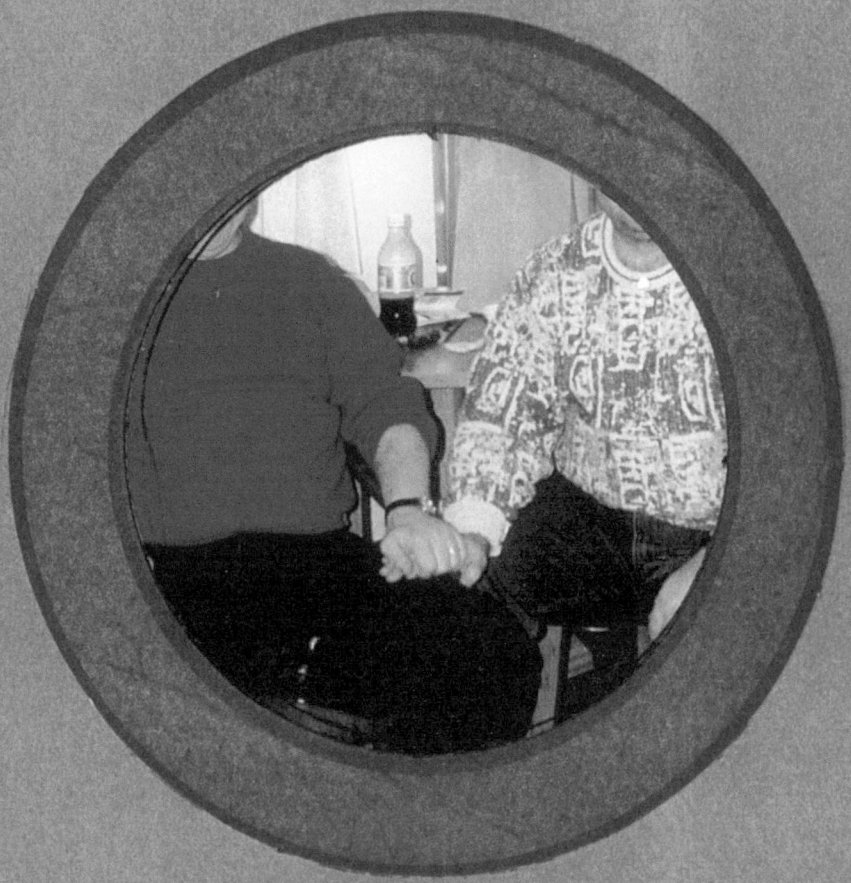

i thought if i RAN
into a tree
it would LOOK like an
accident

THE BUTTERFLIES
ARE GONE.

if i had a time machine
i would not kill hitler
or meet jesus
i would take you to the movies.

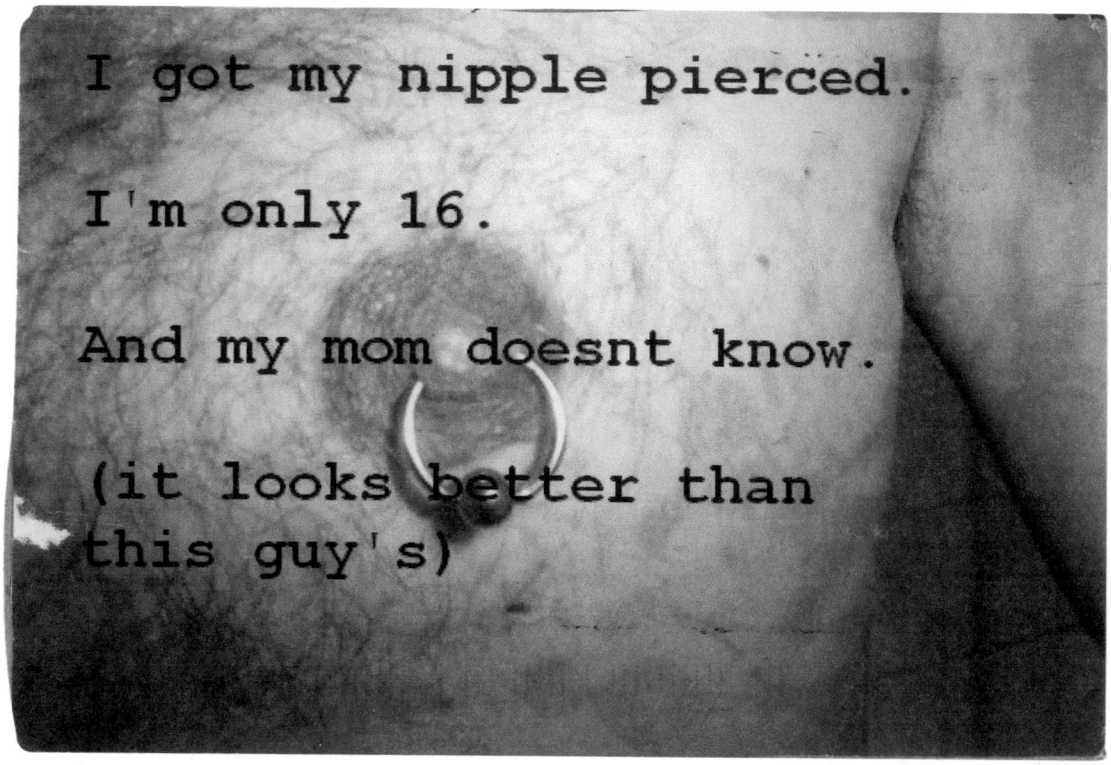
I got my nipple pierced.
I'm only 16.
And my mom doesnt know.
(it looks better than
this guy's)

Finally found my way
SURPRISE!
ADOLECENCE IS NOT AN EXITING ADVENTURE
IT'S ACTUALLY VERY BORING
AND LONLIER THAN YOU COULD EVER IMAGIN

I haven't told
you everything.

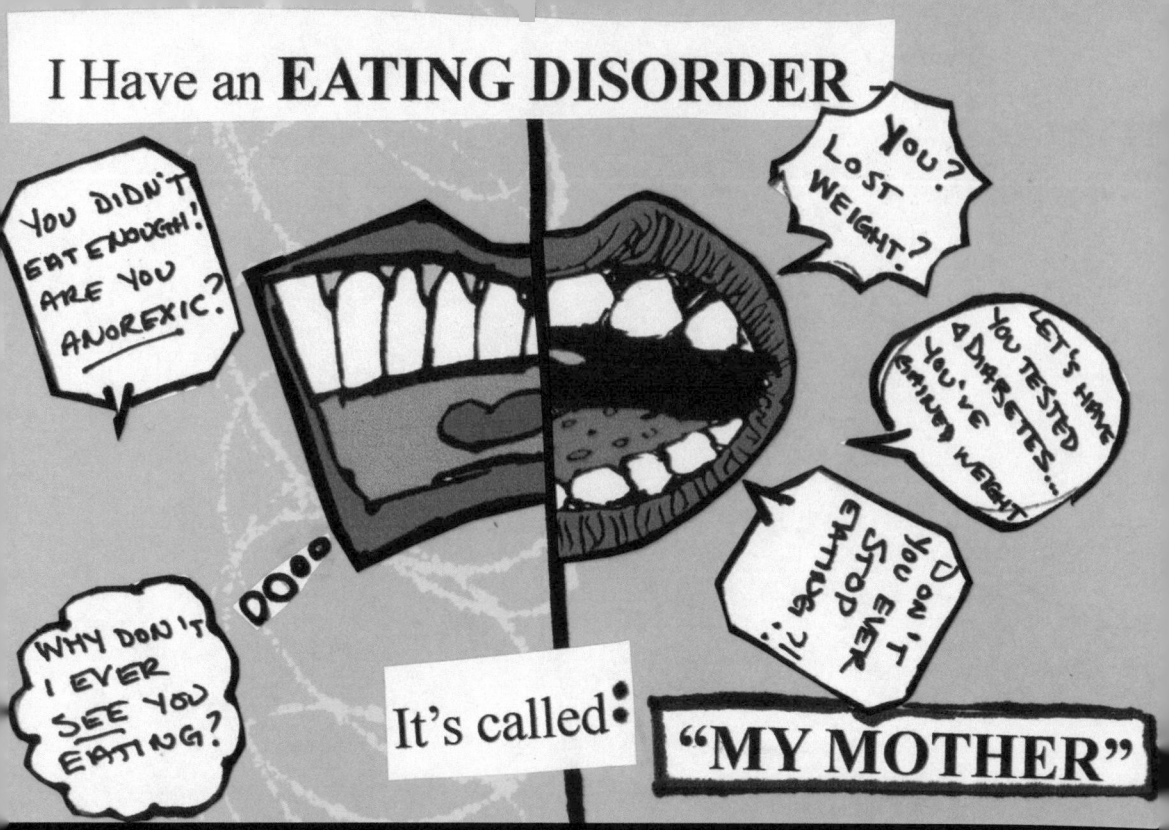
I Have an EATING DISORDER
YOU DIDN'T EAT ENOUGH! ARE YOU ANOREXIC?
YOU? LOST WEIGHT?
LET'S HAVE YOU TESTED 4 DIABETES.. YOU'VE GAINED WEIGHT
DON'T YOU EVER STOP EATING?!
WHY DON'T I EVER SEE YOU EATING?
It's called:
"MY MOTHER"

let me tread my own path
don't worry i will be fine

this year,
i overcame my
fear of sleeping
with the closet
open. i'm 22.

i WISH i were
addicted to
things...

so i
could
blame
THEM for
why i'm so
messed up.

i kept the letter your boyfriend wrote for you and put it in my room so someone might find it and think that someone is in love with me...

I miss you
I love you
but I dont know who you are

YET

Maybe this isn't what she/he wants or
immediately wanted to say what I told myself
School doesn't last forever . . . it will not

needs to hear, but when I read the card I
for those four years: It's going to be okay.
define your life.

—Japan

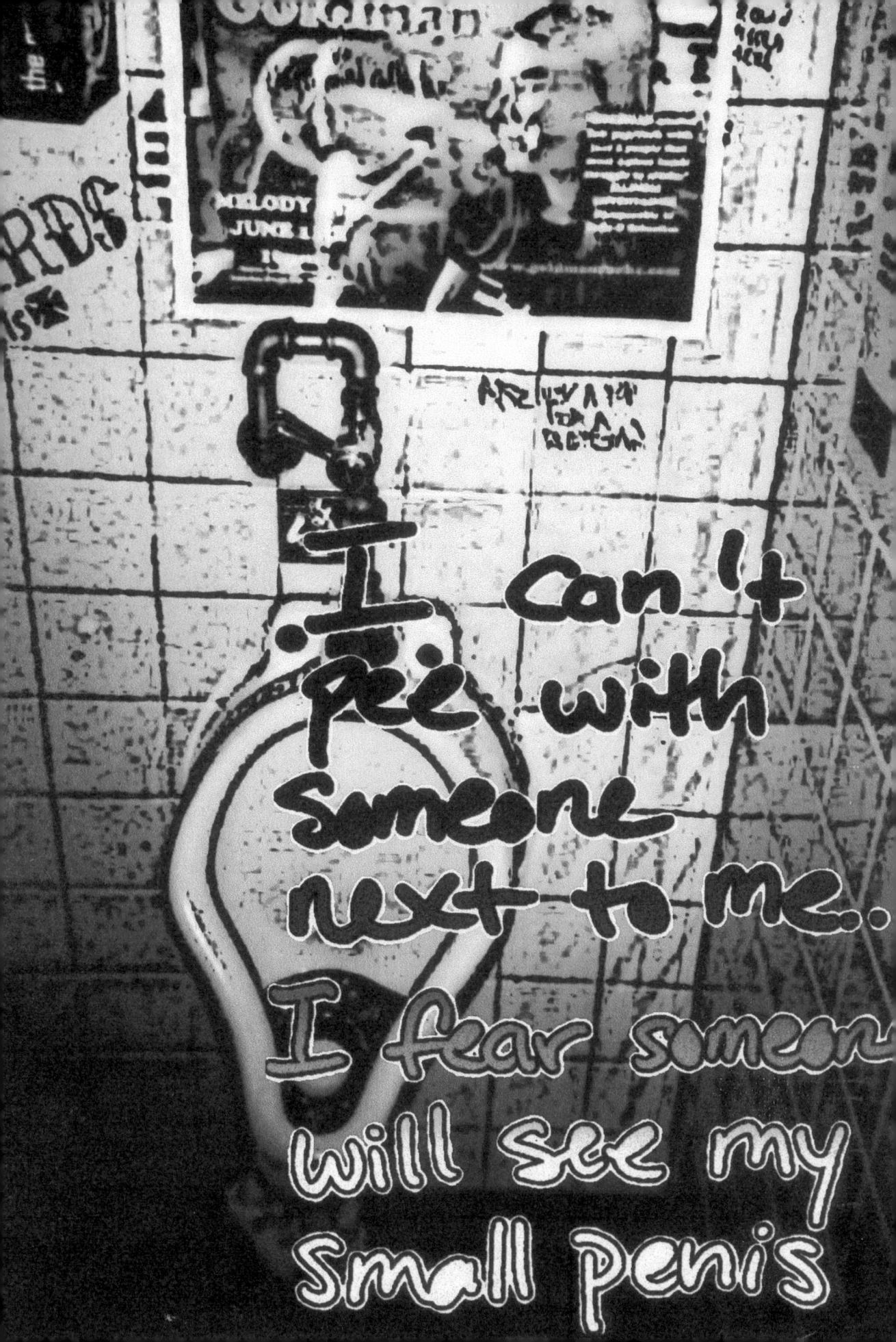
I can't pee with someone next to me.
I fear someone will see my small penis

I'm afraid that deep down I am truly unworthy of another person's love.

616.85
B
Bradshaw, John, 1933-
Healing the shame that binds you /
John Bradshaw. -- Deerfield Beach, Fla.
: Health Communications, c1988.
ix, 245 p. : ill.
ISBN 0-932194-86-9

NPsP 19 FEB 90 18162520 VNFAsl 88-21228r89

People don't change...
They just find new ways
to lie to you...

As a little Girl I
Dreamed of flying
one of these.
Now I Just flirt
with men in the military
cause they have the future
my parents would never
let me have
F-18
et

MILK
MILK

I accidentally stumbled across my dad's porn stash...

And it turns out that he has a fetish.

this
will give me nightmares
for a
week.

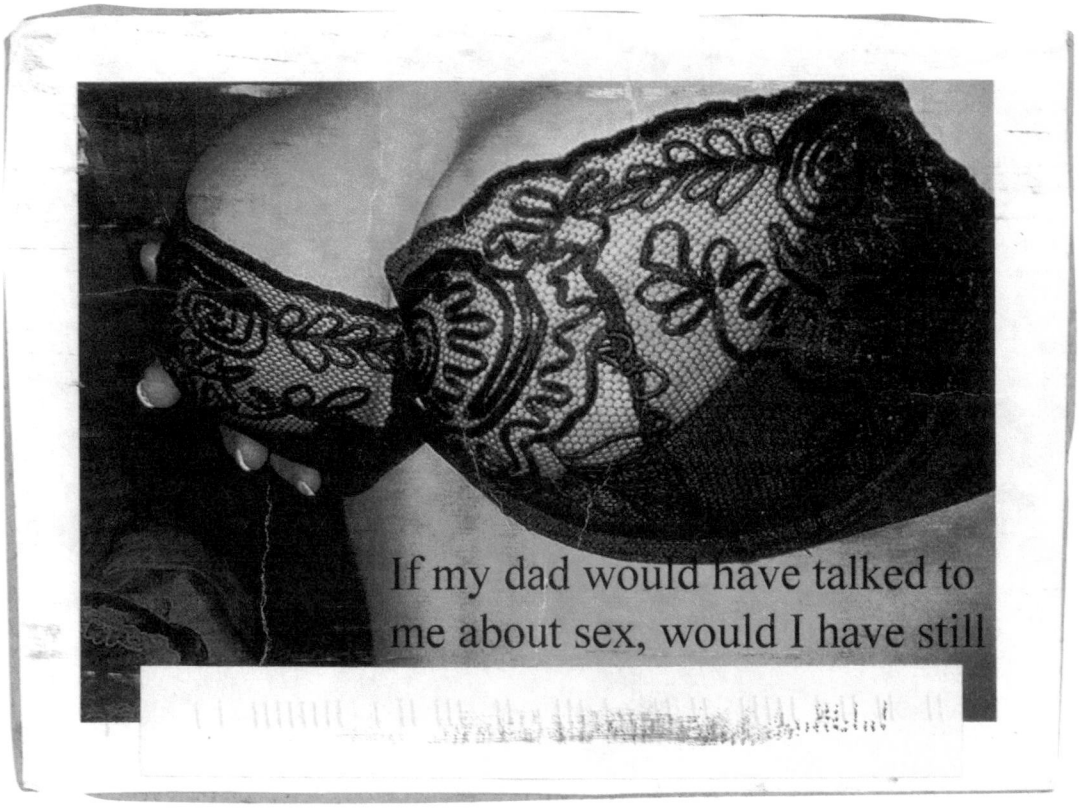
If my dad would have talked to
me about sex, would I have still

I wish Death upon my chemistry teacher

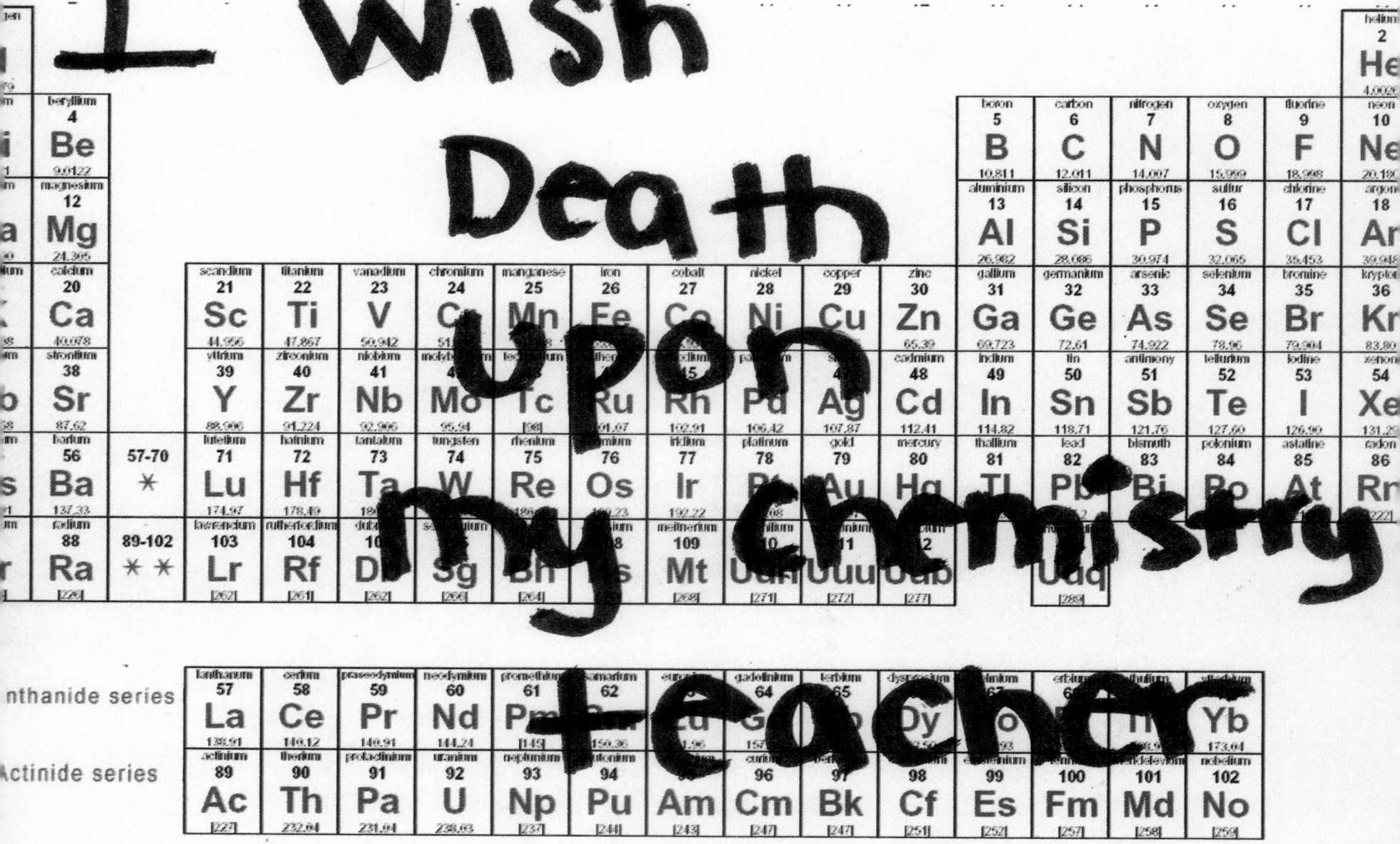

I know I have a secret inside me,
but I don't know what it is.

When I was fourteen I tried to commit suicide with a razor, then with pills. Now that I am thirty I understand that my teenage problems were resolvable. I would have missed out on things like being a parent, my nephews, getting my first tattoo, learning to ride a motorcycle and falling in love. Even though I will have these scars on my arms for life I am glad I didn't die.

When I was a kid I thought
I was
Special
Now
I'm not
so sure

I

dream i had once i was away up in the sky Blue,everything:
was made of brass hangIng from strings (or)someThing i was
ar it was COOL didn't have anything on and I was hot all
or was

anonymously

mail

here's just room for me in You
goes into your Little Stomach My legs are in your legs Your
e around; my head fits(my head)in your Brain—my,head's
ning
)with your head.all big

e.e. cummings

poems

to people

I recorded my cat
meowing on a minicassette
and hid it in the school
library on "play".

I steal photographs from my Grandma.
...Because I find it hard to see things from her point of view

I finally know
who I am.

I HOPE
TO NEVER
FORGET
SAN JUAN PR 009
26 APR 2006 PM 2 T

one of these days I'll find a home

I just finished up seven years working at a mail center, and over that time I would come across PostSecret postcards, and take the time to read them. Some were funny, some touching, some heartbreaking. But every time I read them I knew I was in a privileged position—not only because I was perhaps one of the first people to read these beautifully crafted cards, but also because I was being let into somebody's soul and sharing with them whatever emotion they invested into creating the card.

I just want to let people out there know that even if your postcard doesn't show up on the website, there's a hardworking postal worker who is taking the time to read your secret, and who identifies with this brave, faceless, nameless sender.

—New Zealand

FRANK WARREN is a small business owner who started PostSecret as a community art project. Since October 2004, Warren has received thousands of anonymous postcards, which have been featured in galleries, a traveling art exhibit, the popular music video for the All-American Rejects' "Dirty Little Secret," and, most recently, in the bestselling book *PostSecret.* Ranked by *New York* magazine as the third most popular blog on the Internet, Warren's website earned several awards at both the 2006 Bloggy and Webby Awards and continues to attract over 3 million visitors a month. Warren has appeared on *Today, 20/20*, CNN, MSNBC, NPR, and Fox News, among others. Warren lives in Germantown, Maryland, with his wife and daughter.

www.postsecret.com